I am a Swan with the night kohl painted

around the edges of my eyes

with the colors of ink that floods

just as wildly from under my wings

www.reenadoss.com

AF377765

Solo Works

To *learn more about Reena Doss' other published works,*
visit her website at www.reenadoss.com

Pearl On A Summer Leaf

An autobiographical collection

Swallowing The Moon

Ballads from my heart

The Last Leaf Of Autumn

Barefoot and falling, infinity is a number that has none to end

Fragments

The Charcoal Diaries - Volume 1

Beginnings

The Charcoal Diaries - Volume 3

THE CHARCOAL DIARIES

IN-BETWEENS

VOLUME 2

REENA DOSS

An Ink Gladiators Press® Publication

First Edition
Copyright © 2024 Reena Doss

In-Betweens

The Charcoal Diaries — Volume 2

ISBN 13: 978-93-90766-39-0

Cover Art, Illustrations & Book Design: Leonie Belle Hawk

Editor: Shruti Sharma
Proofers: Magic Megan and Brandy Lane

All rights reserved. This edition may only be distributed by the author. The contents of this book are the author's perceptions, observations, and insights, based on her individual experiences. Any resemblance to real persons is unintended and should not be inferred. The author asserts her moral rights. No part of this book may be reproduced in any form, or by electronic or mechanical means, including information storage and retrieval systems, without written permission from the author, with the only exception being made for a reviewer who may quote brief passages in a review. Disclaimer: The views and opinions expressed by the author are personal and do not represent those of Ink Gladiators Press®, its staff, communities, or affiliates, unless explicitly stated.

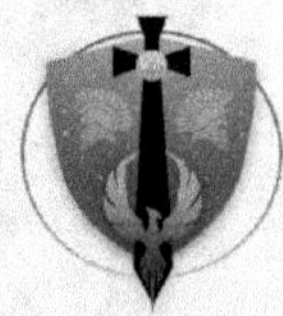

Ink Gladiators Press®

Publishing and promoting warriors on life's battlefield

Founded in 2019 | Bangalore, India
www.inkgladiatorspress.com

My Beloved Weaver

I keep you at the center of my heart because without you, how can it balance on the ocean of ink that needs you to calm what none can, to give me joy in the storm and reminders to smile at adversity as well as laugh beguilingly when happiness finds me.

The Love Of My Life

You are the one who has been gifted with the tools to sail my heart in the direction that allows it the freedom to adventure with you, always at its helm.

The Communities, Organizations and Groups On Instagram

It is impossible to name each of you here, but you know exactly who you are and I just wanted to say this—Thank you very much. I appreciate you all. You inspire me.

The Charcoal Diaries is a set of little books meant for the well-being of your soul. Including the **Love Notes For You** section, the pieces have been placed according to the alphabetical order of the titles. Each piece is a standalone voice in a collection of voices that touch on different themes, social topics and world related issues.

About In-Betweens

Welcome to *Volume 2* of *The Charcoal Diaries*. Thank you for choosing to read *In-Betweens*. This book will open you to the miracle of what happens when you allow everything to stand still, not for the purpose of stagnancy, but to listen to the beat of your own heart so you can take action about what truly matters.

Where does it point?

What compass takes you to the paths you know are for you?

Why do you choose them to be yours?

Allow the questions to simmer on a low flame and let it build up its speed from your heart—not from a lack of something within, but from a desire to add love into the places where love was taken away from you.

In-Betweens

Love Notes For You

Acknowledgements

I stopped numbering my pages.
Infinity seems to be a better number and my story is still unwritten.
Besides, I do like its symbol a lot—a sleeping 8.

∞

Scribbles

Letter from the author

Dear Reader,

There are many stories in the human heart built from every moment, experience, and person we ever met. But it is only at the right time, and if we are willing, that the world we create within us opens to the rest of the world outside us, for others to find their stories within the worlds within them too.

A dream should never be built with the aim of wealth, fame, or earning respect from those who never gave it to you when they should have treated you in the way that they wished to be. Wealth, fame, and respect are perspectives, yet paradoxically, they tag along as sidekicks to the affairs of your dream. They are already measured by the world as wanted. But if you look at them through the eyes of your dream, you will see that the worlds in between will never collide—because you have allowed them to deny your very matter of existence. But when you remove them from the focus of your dream, you will find that they will orbit around you instead, just like the planets, knowing that your dream is their reality, and for them to be a part of it, they must ask to join in.

This is a cycle of life, because it is what takes place in the in-betweens that shape us into the suns that we were created to be.

May the quill of hope find you in the dark!

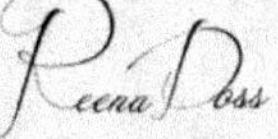

Add More Of You, Please

We were born to add what was lacking into the world, not blend with its problems.

We were each created to be a very important solution, formed in our humaneness with aching detail and sent here to be trained from the time of conception to the time we leave. Learn how to express, plant, and feed its growth, especially during those times when we did not receive what we were naturally and generously blessed with.

Really check in with yourself as a priority. See your path. Make the time. Create space. Heal. Find gifts in the wounds. It will be worth it. Carrying out what you were called to do will feel like failure crashing into you repeatedly. You will often feel like giving up. Be patient with yourself in a way no one else will, but God already is. Spoken and unspoken expectations will try to take you down when you least expect it. Remember the sacrifices you made, the indignities you endured, and the humiliation you accepted when you understood your purpose. This struggle is necessary for the heart to become flesh.

It is those we think should know who we are that are not privileged to see what those who actively join you on your true path see being born from the ashes. It is those who already gave up on what they couldn't understand that you will learn to appreciate in yourself first and then gift to others. It is those who wanted a lesser story for you that can never see your real purpose in God's hands.

It's okay. Everything and everyone you met was part of your journey into the now. Feel the depth of this. Know that you are worthy and erupt. Bloom…

There are living stories of grace all around us, so even in the midst of evil, be strong by standing up for what is good, by protecting what is innocent, and by offering grace to those who need it, simply because you received it through random acts of kindness by strangers, from tender hands that changed your life, and from people who didn't have to but did.

Time is limited but everything good that we do is all accounted for in the Book of Life so ADD more of YOU, please. With integrity. With intelligence. With intention. There will come a time when we will be answerable for the way we used our gifts, our talents, and our abilities. Use them well. Watch how it multiplies into the world.

Don't numb or lose your voices with the voices of others

Reena Doss

Against Prejudice

Prejudice towards a people is what creates wars

When anyone asks you to hate
or spread dissent towards a collective people
after judging an individual
or minority group's behavior
as a cause for their being labelled
(be it their race, community, nationality,
belief system, gender or views), what
should your answer be?

Learn to have the courage to say No
to walk away from a room
that is using worldly intelligence
to forget their hearts are human
and to refuse to accept bias
from those who demand your loyalty

I see this happening in close circles
where the heart's truth
is being overwritten by those who believe
their past experiences should be ours

I'm not sorry to say this
because I do not think one's experience
is on the same wavelength as prejudice

The Charcoal Diaries – Volume 2

Wisdom from experience has nothing to do
with treating a whole people/nation as wrong

You must be okay to be disliked and hated
when you choose love as the answer
to what you do with your gifts,
to what is important for others
who need your voice
and when you need to be authentic
to your personal integrity,
not the toxic waste heaped on you
by those you want to please

Be okay with standing by your convictions
Sometimes you may not be aware
how hatred is a projection of what you feel
or see within yourself and in another
It is a darkness in your own heart
that you must pull out before you use hatred
to avoid unresolved pain, irrational fears
and resort to unthinkable deeds

Hatred begins in whispers
in forwards and in jokes
Be careful what you promote
Be clear in your voice of truth

Don't use your hatred or unacceptance
or productivity to vandalize the heritage

Reena Doss

of a culture that feels, thinks and believes
in different things than you
with your mouth, words or hands

Heal yourself first, then room for
condemnation will no longer exist

Curiosity, kindness and encouragement
will be the wells that you draw from
because its source is love
and love comes from God
which is meant to be passed
through us to others

Spread love

All Life Matters

Abortion is a complex issue and approaching it with empathy requires a lot of listening to stories you may not necessarily agree with, but if you sit beside the hurt, you can understand their pain. This is why, I respectfully, encourage consideration of all life's value.

Over the years, many stories of the death of innocence have found a place of comfort in the hands of my heart. I listened, cried and held the broken. I always wondered why God sent them to me because I did not know what to do or say except be there for them even if they forgot about me later. Yet so many of their stories haunt me because I felt each one so deeply that I have spent many nights crying, grieving and praying for souls I did not know existed until I learned of their existence. Perhaps that's why I tell people who make a difference in mine how glad I am that they exist. But now the time has come to release the sad stories that aren't mine to keep so they can find the light and no longer remain buried in my chest.

There was a story of a young girl aborting her child because she feared her family's disappointment. There was the mother who found a shocking receipt that her daughter wanted her to find because she didn't know how to tell her. There is a mother who kept silent because she didn't want to deal with the impact it would have on her perfect idea of family. There is a family that lost their child because they forced an abortion and then did not know where to go for medical help because there were no centers available to save her.

Reena Doss

There is a girl who looked for comfort in alcohol and bad company because she felt rejected by her family who couldn't see her regret nor did they ask her questions about what she cried about. There is a couple who knew what their daughter was going to do but guilt tripped another child of theirs into unknowingly helping her fix the problem.

There is the boy who had no say in the abortion of his child and chose drugs to deal with the pain of loss. There is a man who had to accept abortion because it is legal for a woman to change her mind about having a baby they knew they were once excited about having.

There is the father who couldn't accept the truth of his children's actions and instead abused his son and daughter verbally with derogatory names so they ended up accepting them from partners who told them it was sexy while all that they wanted to do was use them temporarily.

There is the thoughtless youth who carved out their hearts by indulging in pleasure and saying it is their right to have fun as they controlled life when it began until they grew up and started to cry when they held their child and thought of the others.

There is the man who cheated so much that he normalized abortion as something that happened when he messed around. There is a woman who was told that abortion is a better choice for her life to have "more quality". There is a mother who cried as her baby was aborted because her fetus died after her belly was kicked.

∞

There is a woman who stood up for her baby when the entire hospital and her own family told her to abort her child because the child would not be born normal but special.

There are a lot more stories and I heard many because I know the world would not. You may not like to hear them but it is a reality of what occurs and the way people punish themselves after going through hell on their own, or committing deep emotional scars to their souls or just to please others, make you realize that there is nothing easy about living with the consequences of taking or experiencing the loss of life. I encourage everyone not to be so quick to judge others, but instead to be truthful to your heart, even as we hold those—whose actions by self and others caused unresolved pain—with lots of love.

These days I realize more clearly why their hearts found me to weep their oceans of sorrow. Maybe they knew I have always stood for— life in all its forms, including them. There have also been times when I was made to agree with certain opinions or thought processes even though my heart rebelled against the louder voices that mocked my softer one that still spoke up but today I am no longer unsure or hesitant as I speak with my fierce heart.

This is why I use my voice, not just for the children but for all those lives who carry the pain of sorrow around what they didn't understand or know they can heal from. Death (not just the physical one) comes in many forms—chiefly among them is rejection, neglect, abandonment, abuse, dismissal, withholding and insisting on perfectionism.

Reena Doss

When you pluck such beautiful flowers before their time, you take away the rarest unicorn of dreams from your own. Children are the beating hearts of this world. They come bearing gifts for you and are never a burden. To take their lives is to forever change your life. For something so innocent to be sacrificed in the name of peace, by humanity's lack of understanding is to inflict profound pain upon all our souls.

I stand for life, and for those who've experienced pain.

We must stand up for the voiceless

∞

A Prayer

Lord, you send the sun and rain for everyone. I know I'm unworthy to ask. I complain so much of my struggles when I am better off than so many others in the world. Help me remember this when I feel unable to forgive myself for choosing not to see myself in the way that you love me.

Don't let my trials, tribulations and scars be in vain. Let them all be used for your glory. And what tears I feel in my heart during this time, let them not sink in me but help me offer them to you so nothing is ever wasted.

Please exchange them for grace towards the children struggling in every other part of the world. They don't deserve to be a target for hate. Save them, Lord. Save them, please. Or take them home to you and your Mother.

Amen.

For the Children of the World

Reena Doss

Attitudes

Be proud of our country's achievements without becoming arrogant. When other nations or organizations or countries appreciate us, being humble and gracious with accepting such honor, praise and respect is good—like how the government and the people who deserved the direct praise already did—and we, as citizens, should feel proud too.

However, I have also encountered a small margin of individuals that react to this type of news in very toxic ways and which I want to speak up about as it is quite shocking to notice how egotistical, boastful and competitive some of my countrymen get during international recognition. It irks me because there is no need to use comparison as a tool at all. Achievements speak for themselves while small minded attitudes like this lack integrity and are a disservice to a country's growth, let alone their own. The need to put down other people, cultures and nations just to gloat during glorious times is not good sportsmanship.

I do not stand with people like this who use the glamour of another citizen's achievements to put down others, cultures and nations just to advance their own agendas and call it patriotic. These are the type of people who confidently assume that they speak for everyone and take it personally if you disagree. They are not even aware they are instigating animosity, creating division and planting seeds of dissension. They believe they are distorting a global perspective view of their country but really are revealing their weakness of feeling internally inferior.

This is also why most of these individuals miss out on the joy of deeper solidarity with world communities and connecting more with humanity just because they base their judgments on hearsay, false ideas and few bad experiences. This is how new borders are created.

The world is changing and evolving and yet we are stagnant because what remains at our roots are a fungus that we continue to nurture. Cultivate your mindset and you will discover how quickly you will begin to outgrow certain circles and crave the company of those with the ability to dive into more depth.

Generalizations don't allow for the richness of open and real conversations to flow. Instead, they become argumentative debates and allow the cause for deeper dysfunctions to germinate.

If anything, History has taught us, it should be about knowing why, not about continuing the hatred that generations before us carried and expect us to uphold. This is not growing at all.

Blind attitudes are blind to every voice except the unnoticed wound they carry and distribute.

Keep healing; don't distribute history's scars

Reena Doss

Be The Cure

Hurt people who do not have control over their emotions in a healthy way will look for a vessel to pour their pain into because they don't want to feel that pain themselves. Empaths tend to feel so deeply that they become the scapegoat or the house that opens itself for the anger, hatred, and guilt that those who block these emotions feel and project on to you.

If you want to love hurt people in the right way without taking on their pain and making it yours, do and say nothing in response except to pray quietly for them. When you do this, you heal yourself and their hurt plus you feel tons lighter. It's important not to give them the fuel they are looking for. Hold your peace. Walk away as many times as you need. Let them face what they don't want to. Some will find another vessel but the smart few will see your boundaries as reasons for them to reflect, heal, and change. Be patient. They did not learn how to regulate themselves in conflict and that is why they resort to these negative coping mechanisms. Put some soothing music if any interaction with them causes upheaval and you feel tempted to retaliate. Talk with those who meet you with love. It will restore you to peace or if you are an introvert, spend some time alone to reenergize. Do the things you love and that come naturally to you, like writing, art or some creative gift that you possess.

Practice kindness.
Practice compassion.
Practice discernment.

∞

When you combine these three and make it a life skill, the wrong energy will either find you annoying, irritating, or fake but in actuality, what they are experiencing is a need to get away from you because they feel repelled, disgusted or even offended by your very nature. Moving with this type of energy in the world will eliminate lots of people from your life, but what it will do is reveal your true inner circle which will be the people you can count on one hand to be there for you—not just when there are good times, but especially when you have nothing.

We all pray for love and the Weaver answers us with life because He is the Author of all creation in this generation, in the ones before, and in the ones that will be. I do not mean that you must go and start creating life recklessly or tell everyone that having a child is a solution to all your problems. No, what I mean is every child that is allowed to be here is from the Weaver, just like you are.

We are all children. Our lives are precious because we are created with love, whether or not we were planned, wanted or even needed by our parents. Each one brings a suitcase with a deep love that the world needs. We must soften our hearts to feel this. We must withdraw from the hamster wheel cycle of needing appearances and allow our souls to speak. We must taste the cup of suffering in silence to see how love takes shape within us before we express it.

Real love looks nothing like what we expect it to be. You can have it if you are ready to welcome it. Love is not what leaves you thinking that you are not enough, but it is in the feeling of lightness after you learn to share the heaviness you carry.

Reena Doss

Love is not in the chaos of the false projection of happiness but in the joyful reality of having your flaws seen and held. Love is not in being ignored when you feel like a failure but it is in the consistent walking beside you through every turn, twist and tale. Those who cannot give this type of love have not experienced it themselves. Even if they were loved, they were taught to believe that love must only be expressed when it was earned according to expectations.

Do you see how the Weaver loves us all? Consistently. No matter where we are. There is no heart that is rejected, abandoned or given up on when you notice how the Weaver loves.

No one is perfect because we are all learning what love is but the best way I can describe it is: it will feel like a taste of Heaven, even in moments when you want nothing to do with anything about love. Why? Because you know your heart moved into the softness of the clouds—by expanding the lessons from the past, by examining your depths without hesitating to see yourself and in the healing of all the pathways—that you now run on, but where you were once afraid to walk on…

All this transformation began from the time you met them and when you look at them, you realize they stayed and that's why you know you can handle anything because with them, everything became better.

Change happens in the long night. Not because they asked you to but because you wanted to, for yourself and for them.

This is why I entreat everyone to not justify wars, death, or genocide of any kind—whether on the battlefield of countries against each other or within the homes that believe in appearances more. The end goal should be more about stopping the toxic patterns of past generations from micro and macro scales.

If you as an individual wants peace, you must respond with authenticity for the sake of humanity's evolution, not with its toxic version.

Add your kind of love everywhere you go; we are the cure

Big Picture Fantasy

As an INFJ, I often contemplate big picture ideas and see things in the way that it could be. I always know in reality that my wishes for the world will never come to pass in my lifetime but I always believe in the revolution of planting seeds of memory because a thought has the power to grow into a sapling, and if that sapling has integrity, it will grow roots so deep that a forest will one day flourish.

Imagine a world where money did not rule, control or demand the way we live. Step into this fantasy with me for a moment: If you are good at something and another needed it as a necessity, wouldn't it be wonderful to give your gifts to them and receive their gifts in return?

Some gifts would be given just because we can and they would be like a luxury to another. Some gifts would be of comfort to help you through life. Love should be the way the laws of the land, ocean and sky should be run.

We are individually blessed with so many love languages. Some of us read them very well, some need to be taught and some discover them during different phases of growth.

Think about it: how wonderful would it be to grocery shop and know that your poetry, quotes, art or some of your other voices of expression would be your currency?

Then there would be no fear of AI taking over jobs that many do not even like to be in. Scientists, environmentalists, doctors, astronauts, writers, artists and other magnificent creatives could all do what they love to do. There would be no borders, no stress about following your dreams, no fight to climb the ladder, no entitlement to what isn't ours. Because every one of us would be committed to our crafts. And in doing so, we will ensure that each one is taken care of especially the young, the sick, the abandoned, the depressed, the addicted, the hungry and the old. The attitude of "why waste your time on repair when new and shiny is better" is what our global problem is, not population crisis, not cultures and certainly not nature. Greed is the underlying issue.

As an Earthian society, we create so much of the chaos but what if we introduce another type of chaos—Peace. Have you ever mentioned peace and noticed the reactions? Have you ever been mocked for wanting its chaos? Have you ever noticed how the world looks at you when you choose to be kind or when you choose to meet conflict with gentleness? Most people look at generosity, big ideas like this as jokes, as immaturity or even daydreams but how many insane daydreams are now a reality? We could heal the world by making it a better place by simply being who we are and what we were created to be. It will take a long time but it isn't impossible.

Kindness is a step towards it, even if it takes
more than one generation to watch its flowers bloom

Reena Doss

Blocked Senses

I sat alone in darkness inside
While the birds chirped merrily outside
I pushed open my window just to see
I didn't like that they were free
I waved my hands and shooed them away
Shut the window and watched my decay
In the mirror, I wondered why
My solitary life, bound me to die
I heard the ocean waves, race and roar
And moaned as I ran to shut the door
I smelled the passing of my life
Needed only this one knife
Its blade felt sharp and was long
As my mouth sang a melancholy song
My other hand held close my bottle
This habit was so difficult to throttle
I sobbed in despair
And raised up a last prayer
Fell to my knees on the ground
Didn't know that's where grace stood abound
Mercy knocked
Before I baulked
Help was there

He only needed to care

∞

Choose Love

My heart is broken by humanity, by people I never expected to betray me, and by my own choices in trusting what wasn't truly love. My heart is also simultaneously being healed by humanity, by people I did not expect to restore what was broken, and by my recent choices in re-trusting what I changed within to be loved in more alignment to who I am. This is often the dichotomy of life—to figure out how to hold the past with grace, the present with growth, and the future with gentleness.

Children deserve a better world than the one we are telling them they must accept and adapt themselves to. We need to change ourselves, learn from them more and add what we see we needed and wanted more of as kids. I believe we can do more with our voices, our gifts and our abilities. Even when we think we don't have much, we have what we need.

I am so many things I did not know but even here at the end of the old version, I am new because I choose love with more depth as I learn from it. No matter what, I will keep choosing it because it makes me value life more. It is the path that has always felt right after all.

The right path leads to grace, growth and gentleness

Reena Doss

Colombo

Ships awaking from their sleep
fishermen playing games on the beach
turtles strolling along and the heady smell
of surf and sand were the first memories I recall
when I reached the beautiful shores of Colombo

The slow steady movements of people
who gave the impression of never succumbing
to being too busy intrigued
because they seemed to accomplish everything
and yet have time for you

I'd lie awake some nights to hear
the crickets chirp and the owls hoot
In the morning, I grew used to seeing
chameleons, iguanas and Komodo dragons
crossing streets like it was a normal thing

The currency was a great economical saver
and seafood was scrumptious
yet it was the love and respect for nature
that surprised me the most
Every living thing was sacred
even the spider that bothered me back home
was moved back into the garden

Aren't we all responsible

to help each other find home
when we get lost in places we shouldn't be?
Culture can be a shocking thing
but what if it teaches you
the best things you need to learn
in order to enhance your own life and others?

Travel, step into their shoes
learn, grow on soil not your own
Expand your roots
then travel some more

Travel teaches you great lessons

Reena Doss

Courage

Courage is a drink
many do not choose
for its temperament is fierce
as the stored years of seasons
and its ingredients are made
from battlefield wounds
torn from within the self—
a brand label
that is notably priceless
in its rare ability to face anything
in order to gain things
of great value

Be brave always

Decider

Who decides whose status is better than the rest?
These invisible thick lines are drawn so high
Toppling over into cultures and countries
Exploiting the innocent and the ignorant
Forming groups exploding hate on mankind

Eyes of greed condemn our world

This revolution sparks destruction, not change
Wanting more is not a criminal travesty
But if it fiddles with malicious jealousy
The dice are cast and one man's problem
Unbalances the floods to contaminate all

Eyes of greed condemn our world

Arrogance and pride are the heralds of vice
The need for exclusivity and belonging
Descend into pathological discrimination
Where skin, gender and nationality
Become the depraved reasons for crime

Eyes of greed condemn our world

Rejection is the foundation of disease and war
Appreciation cancels out revenge and debt

Reena Doss

True acceptance begins in the way we see
If one man can contaminate the world
Then it needed only one to change its view
For the rest to transform perceptions

Eyes of greed condemn our world

The conjoining minds of mankind

Demolitions

None of us knows how wars affect children or what the future will reap with the kind of cruelty this world has sown. Please do not continue to let silence be a choice when the lives of children are at stake. They are more precious than worrying about who started this war and which side was more right or wrong.

There is nothing right about the massacre of children. I don't understand how people can get so focused on deeper agendas and conspiracies when the lives of the innocent are being taken without any consideration. I can't believe I have to write about this truth but I will because I know adding my voice every day is important.

Most of the world is focused on discussing who started this or why this slaughter is understandable or not and whether Gaza being demolished into non-existence deserves it when in truth, everyone should be doing their best to speak up for the innocent—the voiceless, the defenseless and the blameless.

We must let the rest of the Earth know that no one, land or country has the right to take innocent lives by calling it "collateral damage", when we (the people of the world) stand by them.

We have to, and we can, be superheroes when we choose to stand up for what is right and say no to bullies especially if they think that they can oppress those who did nothing to anyone except happen to exist like beautiful rare flowers in a field.

Reena Doss

This is what history will one day say: "Oh, no one saw them growing there…" not "most chose to turn a blind eye while the flames consumed these budding flowers". What is the point of a casual account by media channels later on about how water couldn't be brought to them fast enough?

The death of children or the effects they will have to endure from this horror not just here in Gaza, but in Africa and other places in the world, are unimaginable. So please keep speaking and doing for others in your way

Your voice matters even if it is a drop

∞

Dichotomy

I remember being unable
to stay wonderstruck
laugh delightedly
have dreams
be positive
get up
let go
live

I remember fighting and losing

I remember fighting and winning

I remember giving up

I remember not giving up

I remember being hateful

I remember being hated

but most of all
I remember loving and being loved

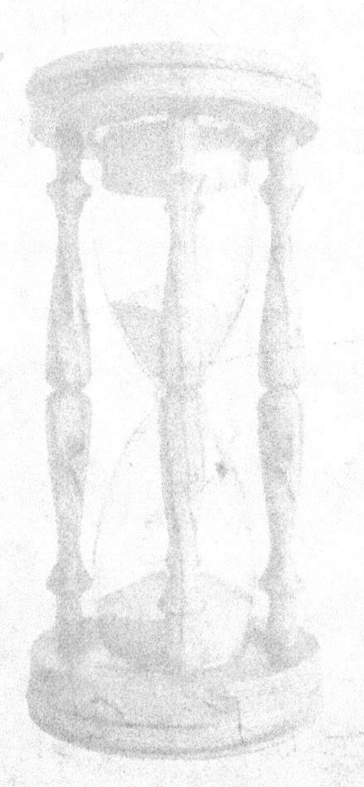

Reena Doss

On those days
I remember wanting
to stay wonderstruck
laugh delightedly
have dreams
be positive
get up
let go
live

Balancing opposites exist

∞

Discovery

I've never been the kind
to be afraid to say no
to anything that takes me away
from the love and faithfulness
that God has shown me
throughout my life

I am okay to be alone
rather than to give up
my freedom of choice

I am discovering
my beating heart is true

I am learning
the weight of my courage

I am content
in knowing who I am

Today is a stop to catch my breath
Today is a smile in the mirror
Today is finding home in me

I am still soft in a world that isn't

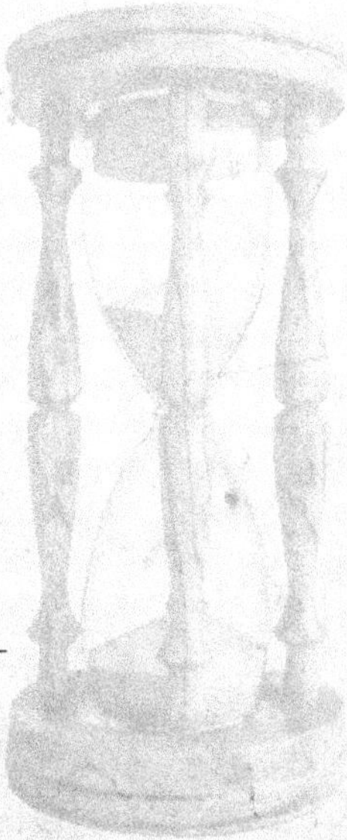

Reena Doss

Egyptian Lure

Tapering triangles set in a sea of dust
Legends of the sphinx and mummies
shrouded in mystery and treasured relics
revealing time's forgotten secrets
and hinting at elusive elixirs
of the dead in their crypts
Some things here are unattainably morbid
yet lurk behind the veil of discoveries
daring all to disclose their stories

Shall we venture into the pyramids?

∞

Evolution

Sometimes we think we need everyone we love to be on our side to have permission to be who we were created to be… We don't. What that need does is, it chains us to them in a toxic way that seeks their validation, rather than allowing us the freedom to align to our purpose.

When you know your purpose is to create, then that is also a calling to be free. Yet we also have a responsibility to be authentic to the ink we bleed. Often because of this, we will find ourselves alone on the journey.

We will feel judged or even be misunderstood but should we let that stop us from being ourselves? No… please do not.

I think once we know how the chains led us versus the freedom that comes with following your purpose, we know why we choose our craft first. A craft is not about priority, it is the very core part of us that makes us come alive. When we are not accepted for it, we may at first think it's okay to lose ourselves to a mundaneness because we want to fit in with others' views. But changing your craft should not be the answer; rather we must evolve it to grow along with our transformations because we are the solutions to those looking for our voices to feel understood, get inspired or to be seen too. Even when we struggle to begin a life with purpose, there is a fulfillment that comes with that realization, something that we shouldn't give up for anything in the world.

Reena Doss

This is why we must continue to embrace who we are, especially the parts of our story that felt invisible to others but are so prominently obvious to us because if we don't see ourselves, express our pain through what makes us artists, writers, and creatives, how can others like us connect, join and resonate with our voices?

We were not created for what is familiar to us. We find our tribe only when we begin journeys that others you knew in previous versions haven't walked on.

But that's okay, not every hidden path accepts every traveler except the one it recognizes.

There is road meant just for you to find,

walk and grow on

∞

Excuses

Strength is a forte;
my heart excels, with pride
showing off muscles!

Aches, pains and no gains;
body retired itself–
failed at aerobics!

Caged now in a room;
activity is needed–
corona virus!

Three entertaining haikus

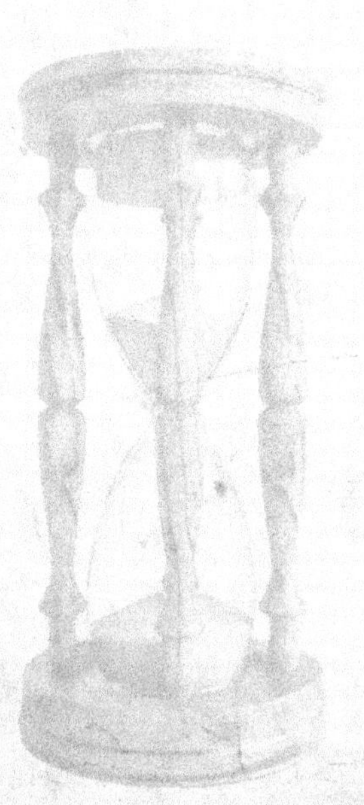

Reena Doss

Firefly

The walls felt too claustrophobic
to arouse my overwhelming lethargy
I slipped on my mask, heated my porridge
and went outside in the snow
to catch the last rays of the sun
The sunset sank to highlight
the dusky treeline,
creating vibrant golden colors
around the porch area
Suddenly, twilight descended
and the fireflies came out to play
I left behind my half-finished meal
grabbed a bottle and caught one
I stared at it for a moment
and felt a stray tear
rolling down my cheek
I quickly set it free…
How strange, I thought
because for the first time
I understood what it felt like
to be caught like a firefly

I glow better when I am free

∞

Fires

The fires emerge and rage
like an uncontrollable force upon the land
A curse or a blessing;
the dice is rolled by an invisible hand

Mother Nature sobs and gasps;
innocent victims get blackened to ash
Charred remains of half-lives lived;
severed limbs——the world news splash

Selfish temporary gain of greedy corruption
where nothing is held sacred anymore;
human beings have now turned feral
saving our planet has become a chore

To fill the hungry, hopeless, and thirsty
we need countless blessings of rain
Earth's agony is exposed in full today;
open red wounds reveal her pain

Normal has turned terribly abnormal
like the season of bush fires
transforming from a natural occurrence
to a disaster zone of chaos and wreckage

Reena Doss

Wash the nations down with kindness
burn our flesh with the brand of Earthians
rip out its apathy and insufferable ignorance;
bring us healing, grace, and helping hands

Climate change has been prophesying
the world on its head in a balancing act
Sad end of creation: a deep peril;
it's time for us to make a pact

As the flames rise higher
cry to the Heavens for rainbows aplenty
let our tears fall to soothe her scars
for the world has been consistently
bleeding...

Nature's spirit begs for tender loving attention and care

∞

First Time Flyers

Heart pounding like a racing cheetah
nerves a mess like a frightened deer
stomach knotted with skipping rabbits
while my brain moved with the pace of a turtle

Having to catch two more of these monsters
before I touched land just felt so overwhelming

Outside, the clouds seemed to zero in
and the world below looked
like a speck of nothingness

How high were we?
My screen said over 35,000 ft

Buttons on the side, TV in the front…

Maybe sleep will help calm me down
but wait…which ones connect
to lowering the backrest?
Should I ask the lady next to me?

But she seemed busy
trying to pacify her screaming kid
Everyone who passed by
looked at her and her kid in disgust

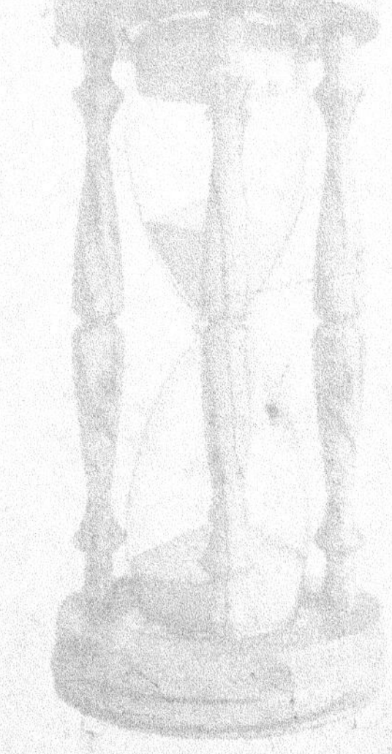

Reena Doss

The air-hostesses insisted
that she not disturb other passengers

Perturbed, she looked
on the verge of screaming
in frustration herself

"I get you, I get you"
I think to myself as I smile at the child
"How I wish I could do the same too!"

The child's big eyes
considered me impishly for a moment
before stretching pudgy little arms to me
chuckling loudly
like we'd just shared a joke
surprising his weary mother

When he jumped from her arms towards me
I instinctively grabbed him before he fell

"Hi", I said softly
letting him settle onto my lap

He stuffed both his hands in his mouth
and tried to speak at the same time
making me laugh

He was funny

"It's his first time flying"
his mother said, embarrassed

I nodded, as the toddler yawned
and fell asleep in my arms
his trust, calming my thoughts
about flying

The passengers, air-hostesses
and mother heaved sighs of relief

I smiled

I think I had just saved the plane

Adventure into the unknown

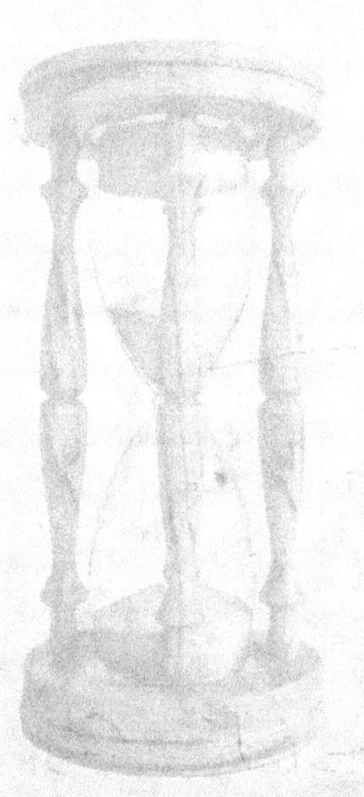

Reena Doss

Follow Your Heart

I've frequently thought about the wonderful people who raised me to have faith and trust in the unseen.

It was so much easier to do when I was a kid and I grew to become a big believer in the providence of God. It got difficult as I grew older and encountered constant disappointment and setbacks.

"That's not fair!" became my normal exclamation for injustice. Believing took courage. Faith was another realm on its own, especially when you had no other alternative but to believe in the value of "you" yourself through His eyes.

"I'm a mess. I've forgotten who I am", I told Him the other day.

"You'd just have to follow your heart then", He reminded me, gently.

A force of habit I never regretted

Forget-Me-kNot

I walked silently around my block
struggling to bring my breathing to normal
as panic threatened to overpower my thoughts
Memories filled with horror
relived over and over again

The Summer's magical moments
were completely lost to me
as trauma became a season by itself
when the heat of the sun shone high
and the days rolled back
bringing back cruel recollections
of an hourglass I'd thought I'd left behind

Positive thinking was impossible;
I sat down on a bench in the park
in a place where many flowers gather
The soft breeze on my skin
was a gentle reminder of peace

I looked down
and felt the tears prick my eyes
I'd seen them countless times before
but never noticed the wild forget-me-nots—
those leaves were shyly
tucking themselves quickly within

Reena Doss

yet still circled my careless feet
ignoring the fact that I had
crumpled many of their siblings

Belly down upon the grass
I paused to consider one
I placed a hand under its surface gently
watching its fingers curl around mine
in a quiet pact of complete symphony

"I'm trying to forget my knots,"
I say, explaining my prior thoughtlessness
but she only sighed softly with the wind
"Forget me not"

Notice Mother Nature's heart

∞

Genocide

Voices of truth are screaming and people are choosing countries based on their personal race, faith and their knowledge of history written by hands that also distorted narratives.

Voices are getting lost in the storms of the ocean fighting for justice. There are many sides to stories.

Voices of death are also in bullets, grenades and words. Any storyteller will tell you that. No one is right in any war. It is just that all sides have stopped listening and have become more addicted to winning, proving their thoughtlessness as right and needing to validate themselves in the world that they come from. This pattern can be seen only when you observe it in micro levels.

Why can't there be active zones in every part of the world where children can be sent away for their safety, not recruited? Why can't we stand for protection of the innocents? Why can't those in power work for humanity? The Earth is larger than this. Are we Nature's Gardeners or Thieves of her beauty? What a crime it already is when crowds, armies and followers load rifles, drop bombs, kill innocents, remain unaffected on demand for total obedience by leaders, networks, and influencers who justify their actions as a right to bring about peace. Speak. In your way—with what comes naturally to you. Speak now!

Reena Doss

Can I become more human? I often ask myself and I know that though I am a collection of so many labels that define who I am, being human means to connect, build bridges, and love others.

Being human is never about killing, but killing often begins with words when we destroy the spirit first. A human who kills another human has already changed the ripples of time. It affects us all, even though you may not even know about it. It fractures the glass, cracks open the ground, and maims the hands that pass on death in the words, actions, and way we move in life in real time.

Several pages in *Night* by the brilliant author, Elie Wiesel, will forever remain with me, but I will quote one sentence—

"The opposite of love is not hate, it's indifference. The opposite of art is not ugliness, it's indifference. The opposite of faith is not heresy, it's indifference. And the opposite of life is not death, it's indifference."

At the age of 16, he was a survivor from the darkest side of humanity. Do not look at his race, culture or faith. See him as a human being, speaking to other human beings.

Genocide is upon us. Speak up!

∞

Hidden Things

It isn't the presentation of what you do that matters, but the heart that thinks about its impact on others that determines its potency.

There are hidden things that eat the world.

Big things. Little things. Things we cannot define. Things that break your heart in good and bad ways. Things that devastate your soul in ways you can't get back. Things that your mind knows will remember forever because it has been changed by what you saw or heard or felt.

The girl trying to protect her brother as soldiers rain bullets with pinpoint precision yet their aim is aimless, futile, and unworthy of humanity's essence. They are obeying orders to protect or take over dicey borders.

If we didn't have borders, would any of this be necessary? Who dictates the lines drawn? Who tells the people of a nation that they should be offended by others? Who incites irrational rage towards countries, races and other defining labels?

The seeds of agony—planted on metaphorical and physical graves— are mingled with tears shed. Will they help their originators grow or instigate hate? Their rain never stops falling in different corners of the world but are distributed to defend what has become old.

Pain is a wreckage that bleeds from the girl's wounds. She had to grow up way too soon. She should have been on a seesaw with her brother or fighting with who gets a turn on her father's shoulders. She shouldn't have had to witness the people she knew and loved dying in front of her. She shouldn't have needed to cover her brother's body with her own.

Wars don't differentiate their victims. Death and disaster is inevitable when this path is chosen. It awakens the sleeping world. The sounds of pain are no longer silent. It is seen in those around them and no one may ignore the way it slaughters the mind.

The bombs are so loud. The songs of grief are deafening. Can you hear them? They grip your heart in a choking vice when you think about the fact that war decisions are made by a handful of leaders that control its consequences in our worlds.

In the end, who wins? The hands that grab all they can? Or the hearts that endure trials they weren't asked to be a part of? Is it those of us who speak up for those whose voices were stolen?

There is so much hidden in things that eat this world.

We all have different answers to fundamental existential questions which is in itself a great gift to share with one another because of its variations. However, it is our responses, its impact and subsequent actions that cause war, grief and suffering. Free will is a gift given to us to choose what we wish to do no matter its weight in good or evil.

$$\infty$$

But when bad things happen to us because of other people's choices, why do we insist on blaming the Weaver who gave us this freedom to choose? Would we like our choices to be taken from us in order to be perfect robots who serve a megalomaniac? The freedom given to us is a massive gift and if we do not know its value, then we do not know what it's like to be caged, we do not have the courage to admit that we are puppets of society's terms and conditions and we do not have the strength to look within ourselves to assess our morality and its codes of honor.

God has a plan for each of us but so does the Devil because he knows that it will bring joy, salvation and healing to the whole of humanity when we align ourselves with the purpose that He created us in— Love. This is why he sows the seeds of deception, spreads lies, fosters our deepest fears and presses on the wounds that make us believe everything is hopeless.

What does the act of creation serve after all? Why do we create things? How do we decide what to create? Think about that for a moment. Then think about the fact that this gift has been given to all of us and yet we are never dictated to or told how to use it by our Creator.

Just remember, if the Weaver knows our strengths and weaknesses, you can be certain, the real enemy knows them too.

Opinions are not just opinions when voiced out. They become consequences. They take root in places you cannot often see.

Reena Doss

It is heard by a blind child begging in the corner of the street while you carelessly speak words that drop into her lap. It is felt in your actions when you don't help an old woman cross the street because of her skin color and her grandson is too late to save her from being run over. It is seen, heard, and felt in groups and communities who focus unconsciously or intentionally on labels which are then brought home to retell by the warmth of a fire.

We are each responsible for the things that eat this world.

We need to get off our self-righteous seat, stop discussing what others should do and take responsibility for the choices we make.

Words are able to do more than break bridges. Words are powerful enough to rebuild them. Words are healing and they have been given to us by the Weaver himself to create good not abuse them. After all, in the beginning was the Word and it was and is with God who dwells among us, in us and with us so how can we still dismiss the gift of free will and our own responsibility to use its power to restore, reclaim and redeem? Is fear going to cost us our truth? Or will we pursue it with courage? How are we going to act?

Ask yourself the hard questions.

Feelings belong to you or else you wouldn't have the capacity to experience them. To dismiss their importance is to deny a self that longs to be held, seen and heard by you. At the same time, don't waste all your time inside its walls. Make room for thought, innovation and action.

The time has come to do something but without a soldier's blindness to everything connecting to authority. You were never created to be a follower of doctrines that are not yours. If your conscience is clear with Him, why are we afraid of what others think? He is the only one we need to impress.

Be a warrior. Carve your own path in every aspect of your life.

Be the expert of your destiny. The experts can help guide you, loved ones can support you, and strangers may advise you, but no human being alive knows the length and breadth of your history, the paths you've had to burn and the battles you had to take part in except Him.

Do your part because that is the only thing we can do. But it is exactly what the world will need to heal itself in the generations that have yet to be born. We were created for a purpose just like how we create things for a purpose. Find out what that is and let it be your guiding light. When we are with Him on this path of purpose, everything bad that happens will give us strength to stand again, everything that hurts will be restored and everything good will be continuously added to our cup of joy.

What are we going to stop ingesting? How are we going to transform our habits? Will we stop trying to fix others and turn around to face our own demons first?

We are hidden inside the things that eat our world...

Reena Doss

Injustice

Hamas were the instigators who started the war against Israel. This is a fact. Everyone saw this injustice but what frightens me the most is to witness the justification of current events and why support is being offered to continue the onslaught of bigger crimes against the innocent, instead of being mediators of peace.

Empathizing with Israel's pain is justified. Most of the world gave their shoulder to them when the brutality of the crime was witnessed. We shared posts, videos and voiced our solidarity. Survivors and families of the victims not having self-control over Hamas' crimes is understandable because it is deeply personal—and none of us can judge their pain—but a nation along with other supporters that are using the grief and agony of the Israeli people to take the kind of vengeance that we are seeing today on the people of Gaza is unacceptable.

Sympathizing from a micro point of view does not equate to the same level of measuring understanding from the decision of leaders manipulating the cost of lives from a macro point of view here. Obliterating an entire settlement to justify the reasons behind the continuous intent to demolish, kill and destroy another city is to condone a slaughtering, a butchering that is beyond comprehensible. Empathizing with Gaza's pain is justified.

Can you apply this scenario to your conscience?

It's like telling authorities that someone broke into your home to steal precious items and killed your loved ones but you 100 percent know it was your neighbor who did that (because you hate them already) despite evidence that showed you who was really responsible. But you can't stand that version because your neighbor is smirking at your misfortune so you somehow feel convinced that they were in league with those responsible for the crime so you (without a pause or fair plan of action) decide to execute your version of justice by returning the crime tenfold by not just demolishing their house but killing their families, their children, their neighbors and everyone in them plus the people who knew them too (to teach others not to mess with you ever again) and you completely disregard the fact that these other lives had nothing to do with the crime that was originally committed, to obviously instigate this type of massacre.

How can you stand with those who kill more than a million and say it's because they did not get enough empathy for the crimes originally committed to them? How are you able to reconcile and condone it with the genocide that is occurring? Will hearts still be stubborn about arguing for which sides are right when innocent blood keeps screaming from under the rubble of humanity's thoughtlessness?

Don't you get that this is also how the Holocaust was justified as right because the hatred that erupted was already sown in the seeds of injustice and laid at the door of immigrants who happened to be Jews at the time (because they were homeless).

Reena Doss

Others looked down on them as if they did not matter, as if they had been asked to be treated less just because they were seizing opportunities and prospering on "their" land. Their hard work was not appreciated and instead a jealous consensus deemed them "thieves".

Corrupt people exist but you cannot villainize a whole race of people, yet it happens and has always happened. The same thing has happened with those who tried to conquer nations through greed.

We judge people based on our history—individual, those we connect with and those our ancestors speak on. Why do you think so called natural citizens can't stand immigrants or vice versa?

Unfortunately, humanity's understanding of historical events, comprehension of the repercussions and the callous view on the preciousness of life has always lacked compassion when it comes to siding with roots, borders and labels. It is not up to us to be the judges of what is right or wrong. We all know this truth deep within us.

Would you take a gun and shoot an innocent child that had nothing to do with your grief, loss or anger if yours was taken by another?

That is a question I urge you all to ask yourself. The answer you get from that is what you need to fully embrace… to know which voice you must speak for. There is a lot of gray between the powers that commence wars when whispers in the shadows grow.

$$\infty$$

Though I identify with my roots, the labels I choose and the borders I respect; as an Earthian, I will choose to reject these very same roots, labels and borders that keep people apart because I am not afraid to stand up for the greater number of voices that are being stripped of theirs, especially when there are babies, children and the innocent involved. To me, God is love. And a God who is the complete embodiment of love will never ask another human being to carry out the sentence of death or even be an instrument of death to His children.

A part of me feels glad when I think that all those who have died no longer have to be a part of this world but get to live in eternity with the God who conquered the closed door of death and made it possible for us to never need to return here. It is how I know that anything that sides with taking another's life—spiritually, emotionally and physically—comes from the machinations of the devil.

We should not be spectators of injustice. We must call out those who think that taking the lives of others gives them a false illusion of power over roots, labels and borders. ROOTS, LABELS and BORDERS will continue to exist because we are each uniquely created. We are not in an ancient colosseum that determines who is more stronger than the other. The people of Gaza and Israel are not a blood sport. Stop supporting those who accept that the innocent dying are a necessary part of war.

I add my voice to what my heart tells me to speak on. I add my voice to everything that I know I am unable to look away from. I add my voice to what silence tells me it cannot say.

Reena Doss

This is what it means to have purpose that serves others. I cannot stop even if I tried. This is the gift I was given—to write from the ocean within me or physically feel the suffering of rejecting what I was born to do.

Who are we but milestones in between trying to speak about the truth but falling short in the grays?

∞

LDR

For couples in long distance relationships (LDR), modern times have technology reaching pinnacles that the 80's and before could only dream off.

The need to connect and feel loved is such a powerful gripping human need, it can astound the mind when you understand what people are capable of achieving what might have been impossible at one time.

Gadgets—like Hug T-shirts, wrist bands, silicon lips, feel them gloves, lamps that sense movement and so many more—were created to gap the bridge of distance yet it prominently highlights how much touch matters to a couple unable to hold the other.

I cannot imagine what couples in a LDR in 2030 will have strived to accomplish with the way technology has been advancing. It is quite apparent from this that love ignites endless possibilities to be.

Yet, for me, real love is about finding ways to ultimately be together and focusing on these gadgets seem to be important only when you wish to maintain the distance.

The heights of love

Reena Doss

Linda Lokhee

Lilac flowers among blackcurrant curls
encapsulated mermaid of Sydney's tides;
guffawing with Ike, her sock monster
and dazzling all under Aussie skies

About the sunflower

Line Of Duty

The saddest thing I've observed are the paths that are being burned, blocked and bombed, preventing organizations, journalists and volunteers from reaching those who need help or stories covered.

Whenever I see brave warriors, caregivers and people willing to risk their own lives to bring aid to those in need, my heart is moved deeply because I know they too are doing what they were called to— with purpose, dedication and courage to serve even knowing that they too may never see their homes again. Aren't their lives innocent, worthy and honorable of being saved? Shouldn't leaders be listening to international institutions that stand for human rights and who have to ultimately always repair the thoughtless damage of political decisions that could have been avoided? Why do people allow those who do not have the humility to accept the accountability of their actions to stand in power?

Being blinded by justifications, prejudices and a history of endless stories is not an excuse because it teaches the young to arm themselves from connection and make the old carry graves of regret and stubborn pride as they sink with ancient chains that bind them in a drowning of suffering, still stuck with rusting arrows and unhealed gunshots of who was wrong and right.

"Let them pass!" I want to scream like a deliberately-misquoted-changed-phrase-to-suit-this-time-Gandalf the Gray from Tolkien's world of fantasy. I suppose I read, see and feel too much.

Reena Doss

I'm not sorry though. I use all my deep emotions in my writing so you can hear, express and voice with me what is really important. Dark humor added to navigate the paths of ethics, morality and integrity can be great ways to reconstruct, recognize and revolutionize how we need to think about what we are told, observe and feel.

Numbness, cynicism and desensitizing oneself should not be options we choose for our beating hearts.

Let them pass

∞

Little

In a world of heroes, heroines, warriors
shield-maidens, queens and kings—
I like that I am ordinary

With little hands trying to make a difference
Helping dreamers reach their dreams
Keeping lifelong memories of great treasure
Letting go of string-attached sentimental things
Searching for lost voices as well as my own
Realizing it's okay to be alone on my chosen path
Hoping to be accepted for me
In a safe place I could call my home

The truth is—
I'm like a hobbit who still believes
in the light of humanity so I fight for its survival
even when I am told it doesn't exist
and one day, perhaps, they will read my books
share my art, hear my stories
and maybe even revive
their own forgotten hopes
passions and yearnings

And when I'm no more, will you please remember me?

Reena Doss

Locked

I hold canvases of thought
yet to materialize out of my library
in a vault of secret manuscripts—
unedited, scandalous, truthful
But I'm afraid of touching them
for I worry about the consequences
of revelations that I might lay open

Dams without keys

∞

Look Up

In restless circumstances
when I've looked for help
I've seen the stars wink back at me
as if they knew secrets I didn't know
about the wonder of things
and our beating hearts

I cannot define courage
because I have been afraid many times
but the stars have guided me
throughout my time
away from bent minds
and crooked souls
who longed to steal
all I ever knew

They are forever there
fixed in the firmament of galaxies
despite the night and day
over the generations of centuries
They remind me of a mission
I cannot yet see but one day
I hope to become
all they know I can be

Becoming me more every day

Reena Doss

Lost Voices

Writing and Art
are almost like supernatural abilities bestowed
developed during the painful parts
of my wretched existence

I discovered how important
they were, quite accidentally
when I was beaten up pretty badly
until I was a rotting pulp
of useless grime inside my head

I lost the ability to speak up
and people walked all over me
thinking they somehow had a say
about what happened next to me
just because I sounded nervous
and unsure of myself

I knew who I was but I had lost the key
to the home that I belonged in

The storm of change
crept into the crevices and leaks
of the battered spaces I existed in
flooded me with words and colors
I no longer wanted to keep hidden

∞

Since my mouth wouldn't move
my hands found the joyful freedom
and strength to capture an audience

I didn't know who wanted to
hear, listen, and welcome me
into their fold

Writing and Art became gifts
I no longer took for granted
I could speak in this way
and I used it for myself
to help others find
their lost voices too

Silence was a choice I no longer accepted

Reena Doss

Loyalty

Loyalty is often misunderstood in its definition and redefined by many people who use its label to do a multitude of things that not only destroy trust but also attack the spirit of human nature, which is connected to morality (that is built on the law of love in which we were created in and for). Some people of course, are not aware of its core nature, but some are.

To understand what loyalty is, we should experience what loyalty is not. Let us examine it carefully together so you can determine if your core connections need a reevaluation, communication or disconnection.

This is important to do even if it hurts at first to let go of what you got used to accepting but if you wish to hold tight to the people who are real, trustworthy and true within your inner circle, then it is necessary to dive into our inner world. This will help us discover where the fungus began, what we need to change and how we can repair or cut so new roots can grow.

Loyalty will not pressure you into changing who you essentially are. Loyalty will not demean or emotionally blackmail you into fitting into another's idea of what should be. Loyalty will not negate or belittle your traumatic experiences as normal events that you should get over. Loyalty will not compare their trauma to yours nor judge its contents as insignificant. Loyalty will not deny your pain as invalid, just because it didn't happen to them.

Loyalty will not influence others you love to abandon you in the same way that they did just because their personal agendas don't fit with your trauma. Loyalty will not make you question your own feelings or experiences. Loyalty will not make you do something that they have first-hand knowledge of regarding what broke you. Loyalty will not call you negative just because their resentment can't accept that you are being protective about others who might get hurt. Loyalty will not accuse you of betrayal when you disagree with their unjust actions.

Loyalty will not insult you in front of others nor cheat you to get off on their powers of convincing you of their lies. Loyalty will not use their position to make you feel less or apologize for something that you know you didn't have to. Loyalty will not ask you to accept being their scapegoat when things go wrong just because they refuse to accept their part in it. Loyalty will not present itself as a getaway ticket to manipulate you into doing or accepting or supporting something that is innately wrong.

Loyalty on the other hand is everything that the above points on disloyalty are not. Loyalty is about standing by you, validating your traumatic experiences and supporting you when others have hurt you. Loyalty will stand up to you when you are messing up, when you are wrong and when you are putting yourself down. This is why loyalty is a rare commodity in today's world and why I value it deeply when I meet its nature in another. Loyalty is a characteristic of your morality or integrity. If your loyalty can be bought by the things of this world, then your loyalty isn't of much value.

Reena Doss

When you've had your loyalty abused, you know you have no one to blame but yourself. Sometimes, we think people will change but in truth, you can't respect, trust or be loyal to those who have not only betrayed your loyalty more than once but have also influenced others to see you differently in order to justify their actions.

You will not find loyalty in those who use or try to buy it from you. Loyalty is only found in those rare people whose personalities embody this characteristic in how they answer to that kind of strength when they are faced with choices. Then you will smile because you will know what treasure you have.

Believe me, a single loyal person is more precious than a crowd. And if you have more than one in your circle, you have wealth that many kings and queens wished for but could not find.

I like to use the symbol of loyalty with the lion and lamb because to have loyalty you must be both fierce and gentle. God is faithful to us even when we are often not. We can only understand this when we have experienced disloyalty and loyalty and know the difference between both.

Things I had to relearn in the fire of the Phoenix

∞

Make Bread

Bread. I can see it. Dough is being kneaded in people's homes. The idea of smelling them must be a dream in the bodies of those trying to scavenge for food. Salim finds a half loaf in the ruins and pushes it under his shirt, thinking that he would take it to his family. They have had to hide because they are all wounded and cannot move. On the way, he gets caught by hungry men. They take the loaf from him and beat him up when he protests. Crying, he tries to make his way back to his homeless home.

A bomb explodes, silencing the screaming background that has become his dark ambience. The red ribbon he had tied to help him locate where they were is no more. All he finds instead is dust and debris as rescuers grab him. Strangers reach for him in an attempt to comfort but he refuses contact and chooses to hug himself. In the night, he is put in a tent with other children. Leftover smoke is in his lungs. It makes him choke periodically, but he can't hear himself. His ears feel like there is no sound anymore. His tummy suddenly rumbles. Bread, he thinks, as tears roll down his cheeks.

I had a nightmare the other day. I was in Gaza. I saw a photograph of a girl who was found dead. Mariam had a smile that made you want to smile back. What if she had the ability to discover the cure for cancer that the same leaders who engineered her death—and others—wouldn't get to meet when they got the cancer that she could have cured. I saw an old man whose granddaughter would one day stop a soldier's suicide in a country she wanted to visit but now refuses to go to, because they stole her beloved grandfather.

Reena Doss

As I wondered about all other life that should have been protected, for what if there were animals and plants that could have restored us during the times we don't yet know. I called to the man with the gun to cease his fire. I hadn't prepared myself for this bodily impact: the universe and I collided and shattered. When I heard my mother scream, I did not know it was her because I hadn't heard her voice sound like that.

Time was immaterial to me in this sphere. Instinctively, I had moved when the man first shot my father and then turned to us. He had forgotten I was in her arms so it was easy for me to leap across her chest, away from where she kept me on her hip, to wrap my arms around her neck. My back was on fire but I did not mind.

The man dropped his rifle and ran away. I smiled at her as her arms tightened. She was saying something but my eyes were closing. I wanted to ask her how old I was. I was so tired. I loved her voice even as I faded away into my world where there was a knowing—I didn't have to be afraid for my life. My heart ached for the innocent, children and mothers caught in this genocide.

War is undoubtedly a fiasco. There is so much focus on how much effort is being put into a failing system that demands the training, disciplining and so called "proper" impersonal psychological mindset in being qualified to take a life on the battlefield of aggression like as if this is something necessary to build in a world that continues to foster hate. What I hate is the way they normalize it like as if they are trying so hard to prove that all they do for political gain, greed, and ambition is okay.

$$\infty$$

The truth is not one soldier, civilian or general comes back the same way from a war. No drink, no drug and no heart can become a replacement for the desensitization or the consequences undergone when you kill a human's need to connect, to love and to receive acceptance. They can dress it any way they want but a life that is taken by another human being stays etched upon the soul. There is no cure for this except to become the cure.

What complaints can I make in the face of such tragedy? I have strength enough to speak up for them when the day feels heavy and the sweat trickles down my neck. I have strength enough to pray for hope and angels because I know God carries us through the darkest hours. I have strength enough to raise my voice, even though the Diwali festivities outside my house make me flinch each time a cracker bursts as I imagine a child terrified and trembling before they give up their breaths under the rocks of time.

I want to protect the world. I want to stop all wars. I want us to strive for peace. When we break bread in our hunger and eat at one table in the long night, we can join hands to fight what is evil. Maybe making bread together should be a leader's order, rather than taking up armor.

Bread must be the solution

Reena Doss

Midnight Loop

Shaded trees soaked in sunlight;
apple green light filtered through
Empty coffee mug with fresh stains;
clumsy remains on my nightshirt

Tired eyes working by the table lamp
Cluttered space of pens and scribbles
typing words out like an express train
refusing to leave until my thoughts unfold

A gush of wind lifts waist-length hair
to distract and I watch, mesmerized,
when dust balls decide to perform
gymnastics on the floor

Hunger pangs and I grab leftovers
Sink of vessels make me sigh
hit the shower, then sit down
to loose myself once more in words

A writer's moonlit world

More Bridges

Each of us belong to this beautiful planet and yes, though we are born in a specific country, that should not be a cause for division but a reason to celebrate how we don't just belong to one part of the globe but in how we should connect to it as a whole—to the people, to languages, to our experiences and the very way we care for, respect and have consideration for each other.

Governments working together as protectors of the planet and making global citizenship a reality would be truly wonderful.

It is amazing to be proud of our roots because it is what helped us know our histories, savor traditions, and understand our culture but who said separating nations was the way to do it?

I wish there were more bridges than walls.

Crime rates would literally drop because there would be solid teams on the watch, wars would be apprehended because law enforcement organizations with varying skills would curtail it at its inception and the mixing of hearts would be normalized, instead of the focus on external things.

However, despite the current state of the world, I am reminded of Mother Nature's remarkable resilience.

No matter how much damage those in power have subjected her to, she knows how to protest, protect and persevere through dark times.

Reena Doss

Right now, we need trees, rain and less air pollution in our cities and I think we are lucky to have environmentalist heroes willing to do what is necessary to restore her to former times and thus, give our future generation a better world to live in.

They are the gardeners, the green-cloaked vigilantes passionately working in big and little ways to bring back the trees, endangered species and who encourage the world to participate in re-gardening the Earth because we are a part of her.

Close the gaps, rather than widening them

∞

Moulding

Darkness is swallowed in the shadows when one gets disappointed by what they cannot accept was never light to begin with. Darkness wears many masks but none of them are the light.

Darkness is our base nature, but when it is overridden with the essence of God—Light, we become eternal in His promise of salvation by living through the freedom of the cross of victory in the act of humility and repentance (something darkness rejects adamantly).

Darkness revels in its corruption and believes light comes from its salvation forgetting that it was God who spoke the first Word and that is how Light came into being.

Darkness spreads the agenda that God does not exist or that He loves at a distance, when in truth, Light travels faster than sound.

There is a deceiving version of light that uses the ideology of liberation, empowerment and beauty to make others feel loved only because there are more darker agendas being sewn. The shadows are a place many exist in and the tool of manipulation bears a heavy price.

Everything that exists in its purity is deliberately twisted by them. There are those who get addicted to the very corruption they never wanted to become.

Reena Doss

The lust for control, power and domination is like the way a snake coils itself in one place, hypnotizing with its flared head, waiting to strike. They think it is them against the world but the snake they feed lives within them, marking its time.

Here's the ironic lesson to the tale that history has taught us: To those who think themselves above the judgment of their Creator, the head of the snake carries lethal poison. To those who acknowledge God but dismiss him in order to continue their path of darkness, the snake will claim your soul and know when to strike you.

Now, don't go thinking that I dislike snakes or that I am against the necessary kind of darkness that brings out the best in you. Why should I? The analogy of the snake and the concept of darkness are easier to explain when I use them to relate to what tries to submerge or drown you through temptations, rather than bringing out the light.

Life is a gift; to figure out our purpose is a journey, but to finally know its meaning is a privilege.

Stay true to your soul, to yourself

∞

Murmurs

All that the shadows whisper
are stuck between lies and the truth,
and thus, I kept getting lost in the fog
that was created to blind my inner sight

When the light pierces through, it is unmistakable
I had to know my weaknesses in order to be strong
I had to face my fears in order to be brave
I had to care about my wounds in order to heal

The irony of wanting the wrong ones
is enlightening in retrospect
It is how you take past stories
that misunderstood you and laugh
when you find your own weird

I needed a heart full of fire
that knew how to sing with mine
so I picked up the hourglass
and said, "Go ahead. Lead on, Time!
I want to meet my Destiny"

Running into the unknown

Reena Doss

Nana

Night silk with moonlit eyes
Eyes that devoured all she saw
Saw that love was the keepsake of the heart
Heart of gold embroiled in deep emotions
Emotions that enveloped her many children
Children with children, to whom she sang songs
Songs of the past that they laughed together about
About strict parents who did normal things
Things that had become extraordinary
Extraordinary ears listened to their dreams
Dreams of lives untold but boundless in imagination
Imagination that was wistfully sky-high
Sky-high, she watched over the landscape
Landscape of her descendants as they flourished
Flourished in the joyful knowing of her love
Love that took secrets and stories to God in prayer
Prayer that I make for her soul to eternally rest
Rest in glorious peace, my beloved Nana
Nana, how I long to see you again

Again comes the memories of the night

∞

Not All Ambition Is Good

When you let the need for power, status and wealth rule, ambition will wear a different color on your heart and you yourself will kill the ability to hold agape toward self, others, and humanity.

Then justification about crime becomes easy (it's business, they'll say), every oppression becomes another conquest (it's nothing personal, they'll say), and a selected narrative becomes the truth (we had to figure it out, they'll say).

This is why I urge everyone to be aware of a subtle danger that rests in your shadows, but becomes more imminent when we get close to our stances on justice, for the innocent and for life in general.

Be very careful before tagging a whole nation of people as "bad" or to "blame". This is a different sort of injustice that emerges when nations go up against each other because then other nations also join in the power play dynamics.

The thing that is not often highlighted is that these nations are represented by their government leaders and officials—not the people. We (the people or civilians or even residents of a country) should not be given voices that are not ours.

Be careful about following the wrong voices in your zeal to speak up for those you want to show solidarity towards.

Reena Doss

Standing with those who are being persecuted in one nation by an opposing nation's leadership is very different from persecuting a nation that is subjected to a deciding leadership. This is an imbalance. The real voices of the people get trampled by those who have deeper political agendas but who are the ones that speak for others. Never let who you stand up for be used to make you a puppet in an international game of hatred towards another nation.

We have all been immigrants at some point in the ancestral history of our generations and that makes us all interconnected (whether we like to admit it or not). This is the reason why we can never say we own the land, the ocean or the sky. We may have earned the right to exist on or with them and perhaps even borrow their best to live a good life while we are here but who said we had permission to destroy it?

Leaders have so much responsibility and when they choose to create the situations that are ripe for turbulence, calamities, famine and diseases, how can anyone still wonder why the Earth responds to this cruelty with her own defenses to conserve life? Why do people not understand how wars have effects on all life? Can you imagine the amount of life that is destroyed in a war? Not just human life, but nature, animals and plants that could have had cures we don't even know yet?

What do the leaders of war expect from the world or their people when they win?

∞

A "Congratulations on winning devastation and rubble because they got it by taking the blood of children and innocents"? Don't they get that they reap what they sow?

I don't think they do. As leaders they should have known better but they choose war as a strength because they felt bigger but what have they really done? They have plunged those who follow them blindly into a space of hatred or where they are getting targeted unnecessarily in other parts of the world.

As an Earthian, I stand with "all oppressed", "all innocent" and "all life" so I will never stand with anyone that says a whole country is to be blamed for the dishonor, for the devastation, for the indignity administered on another nation. Their leaders, yes. Never "all" the people of a nation.

Please stand up for life, not along the pathways of a future that leads to more death

Reena Doss

Of The Earth

Is there a difference between the seas, the land and the Ocean?

Seas touch the countries of the world. Countries are another name for borders on land. Seas teach us how to connect with what humanity has divided. None are still able to define the number of seas for land and water shift constantly, a subtle reminder that the Earth cannot be controlled by the laws of man. Humanity is foolish to believe that the Earth was given to them to mold into what they wanted it to be.

Have we forgotten that we are its protectors?

Have we forgotten that we are its guardians?

Have we forgotten that we were supposed to nourish and nurture it?

New seas and land appear as the old sink, evaporate or merge into the next. Seas are a marvel but they are only a hint of what the Ocean is like. There is only one global Ocean conveyor belt, named differently when found in regions where it travels.

Seas are the bridges between land and Ocean, the soft space between what is certain and what is uncertain, the riding truth between the woodland mustang and the wild stallion, the intertwining flow between the waves and the storms.

∞

Land is not as safe as one might suppose for it is ruled by the deep currents of the Ocean and destroyed simultaneously by the actions of humanity. Seas protect the land from the Ocean yet they jump into the arms of the Ocean's depth as it lifts them high and speaks to the sky in tongues we call Thunder and Lightning. Thunder, so loud it sends shivers down the spine and Lightning, so bright it dazzles the eye of the beholder.

Seas are indulgent, moody and loud when humanity claims what the land touches, holds and loves. Names of belonging given to the land, seas or ocean do not make them feel chained for they know that they are already free and can take what tries to take them if they so choose. Causing havoc is a self-discipline they practice while creating beauty is an art they have perfected. They answer to the hands that created the Earth and give us exactly what we sow.

There is a difference between the seas and the Ocean. Seas are travelers, explorers and adventurers in their hunger for seeing and feeling everything but the Ocean is unfathomable, mysterious and loyal in its love for the wild, the unknown and the tame. The Land is defined and undefined.

Seas, Ocean and Land. We are a song between the three for we are souls that bleed, weep and heal what is elemental in us.

There is a difference and only one Earth sung saga

Reena Doss

Outrage

When will she awake?
Doesn't she know what time it is?
I'm hungry and my teeth are itchy!

I wish I were fully grown
so I can break free to take to the skies
spread my fearsome wings
and rain fire for miles around
without having to always wait
for her to come along

Who is she anyway
to tell me what to do?

I could melt these chains
and her bones for daring
to keep me tied in this room!

I was created to teach humans to behave
not let them try to master my strength

She calls this protection!
I call it control!

She stirs at last but I feel quite annoyed
Her great big eyes soften when she looks at me

I can hardly contain all that I feel
I'm about to burst into fiery flames

She giggles and I am lost
Whom should I appeal?

Our blood contains
centuries of memories
Destroying humans
seems the best plan

Why then do I want to
protect her instead?
I think there's something wrong
in my head!

She's getting up
and coming toward me—
this silly little human!

It's okay.
It's time to show her
who is the actual boss!

I'll huff and I'll roar…
But oh no, it's only smoke!
Ha, but that broken chair's
certainly not a joke!

Reena Doss

I'm still not yet grown
but when I am five
you can be sure
that I'll take what is mine
and out the door I'll go

She giggles again and laughs
and hugs me quite tight
I'm overpowered with love
because she thinks I'm a dove

If all battles were won like this
these chains will be my bliss!
She's not like the rest—
my sweet human is the best!

Tasty mouse treats
and that piece of debris to chew
off that now legless chair

Inside a baby dragon's thoughts

∞

Peace

Be a Fire Heart, enflame yourself with the truth in your soul. Let love free you so you can break chains in the history, psychology, chemistry, physics, biology, and sociology of unhealthy patterns.

To do this, you must feel your heart like a child would. It might seem strange to do but that's how you find the cactus spikes grown so you can make space to soften yourself as well as keep the lessons as gifts to lead you more into the lusher valleys of love, rather than fear it.

Peace is about not needing to act like everything is okay. Peace is about forgiving yourself and holding yourself accountable to what you allowed because you were still learning how to speak.

Peace is about acceptance of grief for the old versions of you that needed to be held. Peace is about admitting your own mistakes and rising up with fire from your ocean heart.

Peace is about speaking up for those whose peace is being disturbed because you know how yours was once shaken. Peace is about choosing what and who gives you peace.

Peace is about feeling compassion for others because you can give it to yourself. Peace is about remembering what it took to know your inner balance and holding it steady like a white lit flame within you, no matter what chaos you face in life.

Reena Doss

Maybe you will not be heard by everyone you want but when you are doing what is right, no matter where you are, God will send the wind to plant your seeds and they will grow and be like wildflowers that hold the sad, the weak and the forgotten.

You are and have always been

absolutely more than a hundred percent worthy

∞

Permanent Loss

God speaks to us all in the technicolor
of vision, sound, feeling, voices, scent, time, and events

I hope we pay attention

The heart of God is always telling us how to love
and one of the best ways He does that is
through colors, in the way He paints nature
and shows us how every life is precious to Him
and so very loved, wanted and made
for the purpose of healing and helping each other
transform into better versions
that future generations of humanity needs

Look at the colors
Notice the vibrancy
The ignorant kill what they don't understand;
we grieve for lives taken way before their time
and Heaven welcomes the ones discarded
while the souls of the innocent are numbered
and weighed against their tormentors
with the scale of the Creator's justice

It doesn't matter if we feel helpless
sad or weary that we can't do anything

Reena Doss

The important thing is
to speak up for what is unjust
so that those who live their lives
alone in the war, may know
how many stood by them

Their stories matter

If this happened in my country
I would want to know—
Did the world care enough?

Wars are vicious lies that can never be recalled

∞

Protect Lives

On both sides, lives are being lost. I will never understand why countries need to control other countries or the need to take over their independence. What is the purpose? I suppose it all comes down to the basic themes (power, fame, wealth, etc.), including guarding territory lines which is fine in terms of protecting, but not in terms of generalizing every citizen of an opposing country as an "enemy".

People very naturally want peace and they have been fed—through their sorrow, feuds, or loss—that conquering a country or a nation will give them peace. So much attention and resources are being given to wasting time on discussions when it should be being applied to ending disease, climate change and hunger. War should not be superficial, yet it frequently is the reason.

Protecting and defending religion to instigate war with others is the worst kind of reason when people should be addressing their own hidden shadows in doing so. The devil comes in many forms but he mostly comes in the cloaks of inciting differences, spreading whispers and igniting spite. They all don't seem much, yet they are already in the framework of our growth structure and are the frequent causes for most attacks in micro and macro levels.

It is beautiful to know the stories of a place and yes, of course, one would love to visit a country with history that we can all deeply connect with, but I will not accept that people's lives in one country are more important than another country's.

Reena Doss

If losing land or relics becomes more important than a life, I'm afraid that the value of the soul has already lost its place in the hearts of a world that sees only a loss of faith.

Faith isn't in things or in the way we guard our passions but in the way we treat others, because it reveals whether we really are willing to lose everything here on Earth to gain a higher value wealth in Heaven. The fault will always lie with those who start a war for no reason other than to deliberately create chaos or tickle the demons of humanity to act like complete fools.

Please do not take sides that allow injustice. Condemn the actions of those in power who do not have the will or ability to hold themselves back. Don't join a majority of voices that are screaming in black and white. See a different one. See gray. See truth. Because there is a lot of it there just like in the heavy crosses we carry, that we think are for us to hold and that we unintentionally pass on to future generations.

When I look to Jesus Christ in my own personal faith, I see already how the victorious cross shows us the way. Did Jesus allow enthusiastic Peter to use the sword during a time of war? Did Jesus use His power to show up those who did Him injustices? Did Jesus offer any resistance to those who struck Him? What did Jesus do instead? He was not a coward because He never ran away. Nor did He defend Himself when He knew it was not possible to be heard. He faced everything like a total rebel and did the unthinkable—He prayed for strength to remain peaceful in the storms, and how did He do that?

He continuously prayed for everyone. He also encouraged others to not fight uselessly but invited them to walk with Him because He knew exactly what was waiting for Him on the other side of death. It is why He leads us into oceans to swim because He knows we can overcome anything that hurts there. I will hold on to Jesus first in anything when it comes to a choice. Sure, I make mistakes. I'm not always faithful to Him, but He always is. I am not afraid to be alone in this. I do not mention the names of any country because I see us all as Earthians (without borders).

What does your faith or belief system tell you? I'm pretty certain that it does not demand war as a means to justify an end. War should never involve the innocents. I don't care if it's been done before or that it will always be the way of things. Change can happen when we heal what upsets us within.

What is it that causes us to choose sides that accept another's life is not as important as another's when it comes to our values or belief system? Not religion at all, but our own scars. Be courageous enough to see this and be "a work in progress". It will eventually save the world. It is the hypocrisy of a need for a justice agenda that clouds the heart of truth—which rests in the way real faith should be practiced, not only preached.

In the end, the innocent suffer, and this just had to be said.

On war, peace and faith

Reena Doss

Protect the Innocent

The celebration over abortion rights makes my skin crawl. I don't call this kind of celebration progressive. The biology of a man and a woman is so different, and yet it is the woman who ends up pregnant. That knowledge in itself should make one aware of the repercussions of having sex in the first place and ensuring that the act of abortion should never have to take place at all. The selfishness of humanity and the lack of self-control, sacrificing innocents not even born…appalls me.

Where is the love when the innocent are being sacrificed, slaughtered and silenced just because they cannot speak? What about their rights? Aren't they humans too? What about their voices? Why is humanity supporting this? Have you forgotten to consider whom you should be prioritizing first? The Children. The Babies. The Unborn. Heartbreaking.

This is a different sort of war on children again, and is a very big sign of why today's generation does not care about children being murdered, endangered or abused in Gaza, Sudan and other places in the world. This sort of glee photographed on women's faces is frankly disturbing, disgusting, and disappointing. I have met women and heard stories by women who have had to contemplate such an extreme act because of health conditions, desperation, sexual violence done to their bodies, etc., and they suffer deep emotional distress at even the memory of cutting out something that is a living part of themselves.

$$\infty$$

So how can you, woman of today, call your body sacred and expect others to see it as such, when the choice to pursue pleasure has higher value than the life of an innocent baby—a human being that could have been born with the purpose to eradicate a disease, invent a cure, or even create something beautiful for the world.

If we want to do what is good in the world, we must first start with what is given to us through our choices to love. Do not choose an act contrary to love and then justify it by saying it is your body, your choice.

Life is a gift for everyone and there are consequences for every choice.

I will always stand for life

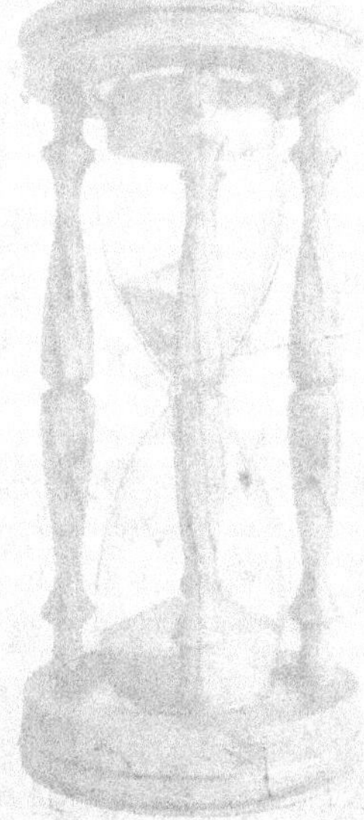

Reena Doss

Rare Gems

There is no greater adventure than diving into the truth of your worth. I respond to boldness, strength and directness especially when I know they are choices. I dare you to meet me in directness and experience the love you know I can give and that you crave for. Conditional love feels too fearful, too unsure, too uncertain and I am too much wild, too much love, too much of everything, very unsuitable for distant things.

When you are used to being loved from a distance because you were made to control that part of you, you realize some hard truths in how you also accept the wrong kind of love because you begin to settle. Feeling and showing love, being demonstrative, is very natural. You must constantly put aside your personal fears of rejection to meet love head on if you really want to open to the depths and heights of it.

The fruits of Love are powerful expressions of it. They must never be withholding in their giving, reluctant in its nurturing and pretending indifference when it is ready to jump. It is quite okay to say how we were taught love is supposed to be is not okay. The coping styles we observed or were given didn't help us connect, resolve conflicts or teach us how to swallow our pride more in the face of love. It's not disloyal to admit this.

Unlearning how we were taught is not a weakness if, in the end, distance, hurt and rejection was earned, instead of love being grown.

∞

Understanding how you were asked to fold yourself so you could be a lesser version in order to be more acceptable to a false dynamic is not easy. It means facing how you were made to feel like you were too much by those who didn't know how to see, receive and respond to your depth.

The solution to all this is to pour into those who also need what you want to give. There is a big difference between those who love and those who use you. Real love will always inspire healing, because everything raw will be revealed. Your real test is meeting those you love in the dirt. Exceptional people will be easy to pick out when you are here.

Keep them

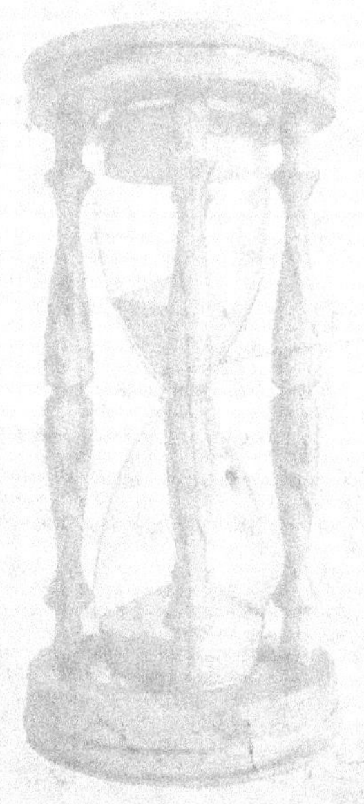

Reena Doss

Recipe

Name:
Impossible Possibilities

Recommended for:
The broken-hearted, discouraged and lowly of spirit.
It is not meant for the faint-hearted.

Level:
Difficult.

Time Required:
Completely customizable to your needs.

List of Ingredients:

1. One bucket list of all the impossible things you want to do.

2. An ocean or two of Hope to overflow from your heart.

3. Seven mountain ranges of Faith to uncage your logical mind.

∞

4. One galaxy filled with Love to embrace everything insurmountable.

5. A broken dam of Tears to wash away your baggage with the tide.

6. One storm of Grace to lift you up from the floor.

7. Capture an unlimited amount of Time in an hourglass.

Preparation of Ingredients:

1. Ingredient #1 must be a doable list of all your dreams you didn't dare to voice out loud.

2. Ingredient #2, #3, and #4 are freely available and do not cost a thing so gather as much as you possibly can. They can fill the palm of your hand or be as tall as the world or as wide as the open sky.

3. Ingredients #5, #6, and #7 are difficult ingredients to procure because not only are they untamed and dangerous but they are known to be unpredictable.

Tip: Setting out on a quest to obtain these ingredients is a must because they are necessary for the recipe to truly work.

Reena Doss

Directions:

1. Add Ingredients #5, #6 and #7 into your soul, mix well for as long as you want, until you feel empty.

Tip: Do not worry about how long it takes. This can take a month to several years.

2. Next, pour Ingredients #2, #3 and #4 generously into your emptiness until you feel them spill out and reach every line of Ingredient #1.

Tip: Adding an excess of Ingredient #2, #3 and #4 to Ingredient #1, will only make your recipe more potent and long-lasting.

3. Lastly, as you complete the last line of Ingredient #1, you will find the taste of the Impossible Possibilities recipe absolutely delicious in its ability to heal, restore, and accomplish extraordinary feats.

Tip: Do not be surprised if you find yourself reinvented into someone more than you dreamed you could be.

Tasty, tasty, tasty

∞

Red Flags

I am looked at with assumptions and speculations, no matter what I do. If these are what people call red flags, then by all means, envelop me in them. When I speak up on my anger regarding casual abortions and at the same time, sympathize with mothers who made hard choices that hurt them in the long run, it does not mean I have to have experienced what they been through to know what is right and wrong. I can stand with both because they are what life is about. When I speak out in anger after I am told that babies and children are collateral damage, I am calling out the injustice done to the voiceless of the world. When I speak up in anger at conclusions made just because I'm not married or when they know I'm a virgin, I am taking their false hints, suspicions of my sexual identity and vile suggestions and throwing it back where they belong—in the gutter.

You see from the age of 13, I have grown used to this sort of nonsense spewing from people who are either supposed to know me or from people who don't even take the time to get to know me. Such are the demons that walk in the midst of us, always whispering, denying and lying to make their narratives true just because people believe them.

Does all this upset me? Sure—it does. But that's why I decided to ink out these topics because I am done trying to explain things to people. If after I speak the truth, there is still nonsense being attached to it, then that is not something that I need to worry about because nothing can be added or subtracted from the truth.

Reena Doss

I want to do good in the world. I want to help others who are hurting. I want to live out my dreams. And if one of them is to give my body and self only to my husband, than that is my choice to make. Your life story of experiences does not need to be exactly like mine to understand my stories. I have plenty to tell and many of them are not pretty. Why do people think that virginity gives others the right to assume that they have not lived life? Do you think I have not received scars, been persecuted, been through terrifying circumstances, been molested or harassed, just because I chose what I chose? I'm not judging others so why am I being judged?

I have come to realize over time that when one sticks to their principles and makes choices that are good for one's soul, it gives others' false impressions. I've had to allow others the space to judge me from the ways of the world. I've been called too sheltered or not capable of holding my own ground, just because it suited them to give my kindness, my character and my personality a reason for their inability to see me as an individual.

Talking about what matters most makes people see me differently. They either avoid me or dismiss my soft voice. But when I write, I am something outlandish and a red flag to the ones who cannot look into the mirror of themselves. I've learned the hard way through the storms that followed me that no one can shut down or drown out my voice except my beloved Weaver. I will keep writing till I die.

I will leave behind forests of the wild

$$\infty$$

Rogue

The travel bug bit my neck, and it didn't even pause to check if I was packed and ready.

My heart beat felt a tad bit unsteady. I ran to the globe, closed my eyes and dreamed about the blue, blue skies. I steadied my hand and pointed my finger, opened my eyes, smiled and let it linger. The place brought back memories of why I did pause.

Two years in this place, where we started our cause of taking off in the night in a bright blue yacht. I would never have done it if my heart hadn't been captured by him. His name was Anonymous—this lady's rogue of Venice. How he dined and fine wined me, before he went down on one knee.

Together, we started the Cause for Love for couples who tried to fit like a glove. We listened and helped wherever we could and did our best to bring about some good. We were not always successful and the job was quite stressful. In the end, we eventually learned that only acceptance is what they yearned for the most.

Most people break apart when they hear the beat of each other's true heart. They write it off as incompatible—an excuse for the theatrical. And now, to travel to lovely old cities and, mayhap, this time we'd fall in love with our vulnerabilities.

Travel was the beat of our own heart drums

Reena Doss

Season Of The Flower

Ah sweet, thy umbrella shadow's cast
Ladybird tied to a sunken green stalk
My feet are not led by misery's past
Yet how shall I lift thee, refuse to walk?

Nay, a green-eyed monster cannot reside
within the boughs of a soul's true delight
Through all seasons, I will stand by thy side
I will defend for I am thou bravest knight

Thou art my pretty solace in this paradise
Light of Summer under shades of Winter
Arms remain open for love has no price
Why doth thine wings not fly but flutter?

This knave is a fool for he will let go
if freedom be your choice to grow and glow

A sonnet about the Bird of Paradise

Silence Is A Choice

Those on the path of war understand the psychological, sentimental and emotional effects on ripened feelings of stirred discontent that are brought to a boil. How does this take place?

They begin with dark whispers, play on sensibilities, unhealed wounds, unjust feuds, your inability to take accountability for your part to play in prejudices, and more. They will use your outspoken loyalties in terms of your roots, labels and borders against you to control you. This is why you must really know what you stand for.

If we don't guard ourselves here, we will continue to view people from biased lens or from unhealed versions that see ourselves as more superior when we are all the same in God's eyes.

"How can I protect or give them hope when I am the one having to mark their arms and legs, preparing them for death and praying I will die first rather than have to identify parts of them for burial?"

"Did I once plan a future for them?"
"Did I once dream of holding their children's children?"
"Did I once imagine I would see them achieve a better life?"
I can hear them. Can you?

No matter how great people may appear to be, always evaluate if their actions are siding with life or death.

Reena Doss

And I'm not just talking about physical death, I am talking about how we refer to people, how we lift or bring them down.

This is how you discern "your voice" from the sea of others trying to insist or convince you that your "hatred" is right.

When sympathizing with families of victims and survivors of war, you must also be aware that there are leaders/influencers in places that were given the power to be mediators of peace or instigators of greater calamities.

The problem with taking the stand of neutrality and trying to play it safe to avoid confrontation or conflict in times like this perpetuates the abuse of basic human rights—life, freedom and access to necessities.

When we allow the oppressed to believe that they are alone because we chose to pacify bullies or even think we are siding with our loyalties, we are failing to realize how our own beautiful hearts are being used against us.

To those still straddling the line, I encourage you to think in a simple way though this is a very complicated situation.

As a parent or future one, can you imagine the vile horror of having to mark your kids' legs and arms to identify them in case of death when you would rather be dressing them up for school or watching them play with their friends and scolding them for not coming back to eat their food on time?

We have—without being aware of it—abandoned our truth, our hearts and real loyalty to who we are….as human beings.

Choosing life automatically puts everything in perspective even if you feel conflicted.

But understand this… Silence is and should not be an option, it is a choice.

If we don't speak and keep quiet, who will?

Reena Doss

Soften

Soften, soften, soften your heart.

It's the only way to truly feel the depth of horror that is happening in other parts of the world. This is not about being negative but about empathizing. This affects everyone. We must validate traumatic events that happened to us for us to feel deeply for others too. Maybe you felt alone and people avoided you when you were hurting. Maybe they marked you as toxic or too much. Maybe they saw your pain but ignored it because they felt limited in how to help. But that doesn't mean we all need to do that. Consider history before you judge a person or event. There are many sides to stories.

Don't go into the place of "It's not happening to me, so it's not my problem." Think more along the lines of "this is happening to my family, my brother, my sister, my mother, my father, my children, my love, my friends…"

Now do you understand the gravity of the situation?

Please don't follow the philosophy of detachment but connect with your empathy. Please don't shut this part off just because you have unresolved pain. Please don't use world logic to promote hatred or use a fixed mindset as a cloak to avoid facing your own anger, hurt and resentments. Please don't forget to remember what you felt when you were broken by others. Become what you needed. Become the voices you needed. Become the love you needed.

Fight being silent with them. Use them because no one else can. Add your ink, your hands, your feet or whatever it is that you do because all of us need you.

Maybe people told you hard stories or you may have had to witness difficult trauma or you may have even felt helpless at the time, but let me tell you, we all have a voice—or many—and they matter. Our voices/abilities are gifts and how we use them is our given purpose for the world. When we use our voices in the right way, we become the solution. I hope you know that we are and can never be unworthy as we figure out this part that we will play in our lifetime. You will make mistakes. You will fail many times. You will go the wrong way too… but if you soften your heart, you will come back to the road that you can create for yourself and others. You are still breathing, right? It is not too late.

The only way to release and cure what bothered you, what hurt you, what confused you or what devastated you is not through judgment, justification—or jumping down people's throats to invalidate their experiences (because you can't handle it)—but to use your gifts (your voices) for good, to heal and to be kind. With discernment, of course. Because when you do, you are exercising the muscles of the heart and using love as your fuel. When you use it well, God will send wildflowers or strays or the wind to those who need it the most.

If you ever felt invisible or not heard, by the time God has trained you and you find the courage to use your voices, you will no longer be. You will be grace for those who once rejected you.

Reena Doss

You will be hope for those who once thought you did not matter. You will be joy for those who once believed you were empty. That is the beauty of when you use your voices with God's grace. It will feed everyone.

So do not despair, feel disappointed and discouraged when others treat you less, or disregard you or even talk behind your back. You see, your voices are meant to be stars that light the night sky. It doesn't matter what they think of you because when you speak through your gifts, people will find the love of God for them in your garden, so keep planting seeds and flowers and who knows maybe one day, there will be evergreen forests.

Fight silence, heal the world, and soften your heart with your voices, your abilities and gifts.

Soften, soften, soften your heart

Speak For Life

If we could all join hands around the world and support the solution that we as individuals bring, what peace there would be, what value for life there would be and what enjoyment of time there would be…

I believe God made a beautiful world for us but what have we done to it? Actually, I don't know why He loves us this much to be able to hold back His hand from punishing us as we so richly deserve and still cover our faults as humanity with His grace. I think it is because He knows our worth and refuses to see us condemned to an eternity of suffering. He exercises patience, correction and love instead. You only have to pause to find it in the Hope a bird brings as it flies above us, in the faith we breathe in and out without realizing how that single act honors God and in the love we discover within us that our wounds once hid from seeing His grace.

Prayers are not genie requests. They are protection for grace to cover what evil is trying to steal—joy. You may think "my prayers are not being answered so I don't believe there's a God" at the time you pray but you have to understand God's timing and gift of free will is not on our schedule. Every prayer is heard and its intentions (if good) are carried out at the right time.

Praying is very powerful because it contains love, concern and healing for the ones we pray for as well as ourselves.

Reena Doss

Never stop praying. Do not let evil think that it can shake your faith or trust in God's awesome law of love. Remember, this time here is temporary so what we sow here is what we will see begin to grow and blossom. Do not be afraid to do what you know you were born to do. Be fierce when you must. Speak louder (in your way) especially when you are asked to be quiet about injustice. Never normalize cruelty. And when in doubt, let your answer to any question be faithfulness to God because it leads to the path of love, truth and a multitude of wealth that will give your soul peace, creativity and joy even in the midst of storms, hardships and things we struggle to overcome.

Listen to all living things… breathing. It is a gift to know we are part of the Earth and the one who created us for this very purpose holds our hands from the time we begin to the time we die. We are never alone so smile today when you think about this as you talk to someone, or feel the trees inhale your exhale and jump for joy in thanksgiving that God made you for them and us, for all living beings he's entrusted to us. Be kind with discernment and have the courage to walk away from what takes you away from honoring the life and the purpose you were given. Support life. There is a God who knows all that you do.

May wildflowers grow in your footsteps. May they conquer dead soil. May joy rush to greet you when you see them bloom.

And may death never be the side you find yourself on

∞

The Frozen Mire

The slippery black colored the surface
Sherry bounded and escaped her harness
I called for her to come back at once
She really was a silly dunce!
She ran wildly across the frozen lake
Terrified, I knew what was at stake

I redoubled my efforts to call her back
My heart sank when I heard the crack
One moment, poised and alert, she stood
Then yelped in horror as she lost her foot
Under, they pulled though she tried to thrash
The cold, cold waters made a loud splash

I walked carefully on the thin ice
Toward her, 'cause I knew the fatal price
The bravest one, who always came to defend
Sherry was my very best friend
I reached the huge gaping hole
I spoke calmly and focused on my goal

I lay down slowly on the icy floor
I grabbed her paws, my arms were sore
I grabbed her harness and attached her leash
She watched me move far back in disbelief
It hurt me when I understood why
She thought I was going to leave her to die

Reena Doss

I hope she never caves
I thought, as she fought the icy waves
Darkness descended on the white cloud
Tired, I cried out loud
"Sherry, I won't let you drown
How could I lose my favorite clown?"

Vowed I
Scared she was about to die
She barked aloud
Big brown eyes devout
She heard my voice wash over her terror
And propelled herself as it became clearer
That I was never going to leave her under
My arms were heavy but fear made me stronger

The falling flurries
Usually, cured away my worries
But today, they just got in the way
Oh, how I longed for the month of May!
I pulled her leash with all my might
We really were a sorry plight

"Please God", I prayed, in abject despair
"I don't have much more strength to spare"
With renewed power, she jumped up high
Falling flat on the cold floor with a sigh
My arms were lead and I wanted my bed

∞

But when I held Sherry, I didn't mind

The hand that saved us from our bind
were very kind, and was in truth—the Mastermind
What a soothing balm to feel such calm
The storm was over; God's hand, a safe cover

I dragged Sherry over to me
Paramount relief, I could see
How the angels had kept us safe from harm
Sherry rested now on my forearm

I held her close and felt her shake
My body had begun to ache
In safety, on solid ground
The lake, we knew wasn't quite as sound

When we got back home
I knew I would not presume
To know all that could happen in my day
To learn, I had to lose my way

I wiped Sherry dry
And began to cry
It was nice to be warm by the fire
Away from the frozen mire

The grand rescue

Reena Doss

The Language Of Colors

Tell me that God isn't speaking to the world
with the colors of the Aurora

Tell me that the innocent slaughtered in wars
they did not start are not painting their stories
of comfort in the sky for those mourning their loss

Tell me that this extraordinary sight
was not an acknowledgement of love from above
for those who stood up for what is right

and I won't believe you
for this…

This is magic that makes your heart ache and your eyes water
at the wonder, beauty, and knowledge of the fire
that begins in your belly when you understand
that such a display, such a joyful orchestra of lights
such an evocative sight of Earth poetry amidst the galaxies
is a whole bunch of extra, extra, extra
just for all of us to realize
our value, worth, and purpose
by the Conductor
who creates everything good

The Northern Lights are a testimony

Unicorns

It looks like we still live in the times before Moses. Babies are slaughtered like it's no big deal. Nothing new happens under the sun. I'm concerned about these factions of pro-choice and pro-life groups that have nothing but political agendas. I stand with unborn babies, souls of light that never got the chance to speak.

I am sorry if saying this makes you uncomfortable but I am a writer. It is a calling to speak the truth even if it is not popular. I will always hold ground with the voiceless. We called Pharaoh cruel for his reasons of genocide but look at our generation—the casual reasons given are terribly shocking! "An inconvenience", "a mistake", "an accident", a "what will other people say?" and "what if the fetus is physically or mentally handicapped?" But the reason that really stuns me is, "My body, my choice" and "Her body, her choice." Hello, um… No, it isn't anymore. When did people get so dehumanized?

And let me clarify this once and for all: I am not referring to serious reasons where mother and child are both in danger or there is serious trauma (sexual assault, incest or other internal or external life-threatening circumstances) surrounding the mother's conception, during her pregnancy or even if lives were at risk as is the case in extreme situations.

People are so quick to judge large families struggling and so justify their reasons for killing as valid because they "contributed" to society by deleting a "burden".

Reena Doss

People love to donate large amounts to orphanages and be grateful their kid wasn't there because they did a marvelous thing by eliminating and helping the world with its issues of population control.

And men, what has happened to you? Have you forgotten that it is your duty to protect the innocent and the woman you have taken in your desire? How could you put that lifelong responsibility of choice on her? Do you think she alone is responsible?

Let's consider the consequences for selfishness and not mince words about it—you chose yourself, you chose your pleasure, your idea of a guilt-free card and the pain you will keep for a lifetime. When did pleasure become more important than life, than responsibility and your own soul? How can society block out the truth of life?

The ones responsible gave up that right the moment the choices that led to pregnancy happened. When you let your bodies choose to act in what everyone in this world knows could result in—a baby, you have to accept the possible accountability for making a life because when that baby is formed, he or she shares your womb and has just as much of a right as you to exist.

I know the current generation feels that they can do anything and that there is a cure, an excuse or a solution to defend guilt but a righteous repentance is far more significant than careless arrogance in continuing to justify and legalize wrongdoings.

$$\infty$$

The moment the blood of the innocent runs in this most cruel of ways, its soul cries to the Heavens and do you think God does not hear it?

Women, you are the quintessential modern woman with a voice to speak up and show everyone how powerful you are. And what are you doing with it? If one of them is to make this choice for shallow reasons, I see you as anything but powerful. Yes, you don't want to be held accountable or made to feel guilty but a baby's rights trump any adult in my eyes, simply because you were given the task to protect them.

Babies have voices too, don't they? But people conveniently like to say they don't. Why? Because they can't speak loud enough inside to tell the world that they are alive and can hear, feel and sense everything that is said and done? Because people have the law to say that they are not real until "legally" registered as born? Because people have chosen to justify the actions their fears dictated above the love in their hearts? Society has given animals more rights than babies. Chris Rock called it. The global audience just laughed, thinking it's a joke, but he spoke the truth and called even himself out. It is murder. Call it what it is and don't hide behind the cover of liberation. Taking the life of a defenseless baby is not liberation.

However, I do acknowledge and concede the free will of every man and woman to make the right decision because all of us have been given the free will to choose. The rights of the innocent must be upheld because they need to be heard, just as much as everyone else who began—as a fetus.

Reena Doss

Remember at the end of the day, it is you who will have to live with the right of choice you make and I only wish for you to never need to justify or regret such an extreme act.

To those who made or supported this choice and repented later, I think you are self-aware because you have chosen to meet your past and had the courage to not hide from the truth of what you have been through. As for me, I have sat with those broken from making these choices, held their hands wishing I could have stopped them if I had known. Why did they reach out to someone who led them down a different path?

Again, this is just my perspective. It is one voice in a sea of many. People may not agree with me and you have that right, just like I have the right to speak on subjects that matter. It is difficult for me to see this type of slaughter being brandished so casually in society like as though it is something that should be normalized.

My intention with this essay is not for the purpose of judgement or to guilt you (as I know many will be quick to assume without listening fully), but to invite you to listen with your heart and for your souls to know the value and preciousness of not just your life, but those of the ones you carry.

Maybe my words will mean something to someone or a group of people and if that is what happens, then this ink spilled will be worth it. Maybe we need another Moses to change the hearts of people and to see the damage they do without understanding the consequences for their deeds.

Maybe we need to understand that establishing human rights and fighting for the free will of all is not an ethical permission slip to take the life of a fetus, no matter what stage it is in.

How many leaders of change were killed in the womb? How many pioneers of cures were killed in the womb? How many inventors of creativity were killed in the womb? Humanity keeps suffering because we often kill what Mother Nature provides as the cure.

Do you think we as a race know what is good for the evolution of this planet? Life happens and it is beautiful. It is not population that is the global problem. It is selfishness, greed and hate that are the causes for such extreme measures.

I think babies are important enough for writers like me to be their voice. I'm standing for them, for women and men whose choices were taken, not for the agendas of adults making choices based on casual pleasure.

How can you kill the rarest of unicorns, world? That's why you can't keep the power of magic with you. How can you kill what is innocent and say it was necessary? That's why you can't hold on to love because you didn't recognize it. How can you kill the treasure you'd never know?

I will never stop speaking up for the innocent

Reena Doss

Upon The Line

Dark—
sweeping black
surrounds and locks
your living heart from
Light

An existential elfchen

We Are Earthians

Am I not a part of the Earth?

I've lived within many time zones, and they all cry the same kind of stories, for people are people, no matter where we come from…

The color of our skin, the language we speak, the religion we follow and the place we call home have never really been in our control.

Freedom of choice is important when we learn who we want to be in the truth that surrounds us.

So why create borders and walls to go with them?

Don't we feel the same things and bleed the same types of blood?

What does it matter where we come from?

We're Earthians I call us—brothers and sisters—under one sky.

Don't forget we're also part water and spirit and of the soil we stand upon.

Born from the Earth like rainbows of colors, countries of languages and monuments of religion, we humans live better wherever the trees can call us home.

Reena Doss

Am I not a part of the Earth?

The planet needs more respite from all the fire and smoke that's been caused.

Mother Nature is on her best mettle for now but don't push her too far!

Nationality by its very definition breeds biased prejudices.

Enough of hateful jokes!
Enough of blind sentimentalism!
Enough of racist endeavors, to prove genes define us all.

Fights ignite. Wars consume land.
Battles are forged over vain things.
Politics don't matter when souls are lost in living graves.

Don't you think it's time it all ends?
Come on, lay down your stones.
Why not refocus minds on rebuilding hearts?

Go on now and plant those saplings.

The wild is calling us to sow, nurture and raise more trees.
Trees are needed in all our cities.
Stand up for them.
Hug them a little more.

∞

And talk to them on the walks you adore.

See how the clouds will gather water to pour
Breathe in and out and do it again.

Praise the Creator for every life given
and let's pray, sing and hope for
the rain, rain, rain
to come again.

We are Earthians

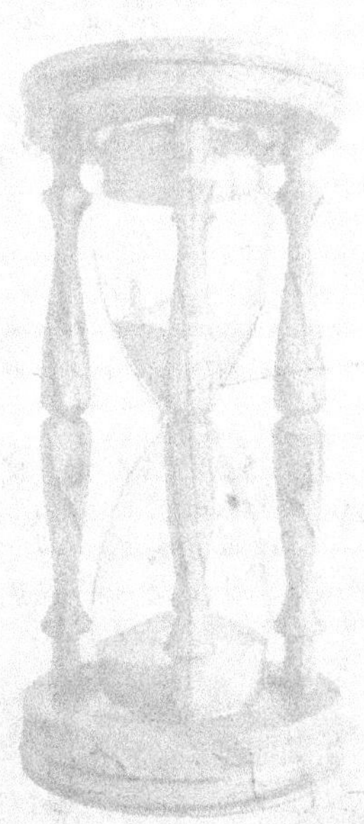

Reena Doss

Wishes

1. I'm quite short, shorter than my brothers and sisters within our mother's range. *I wish I was tall*

2. Despite us being many, I feel alone with water keeping me from meeting them all. *I wish I was connected*

3. All day long I listen to everyone living on me speak, but when it's my turn, they say it's time for sleep. *I wish I was heard*

4. They don't notice the stars, the moon and the sun any more. They even forget to look out for rainbows after it rains.
I wish they could see

5. I protect them from the merciless wind; I don't mind if I'm the one who gets the scars. Could you help support my uprooted tree?
I wish I could fix it

6. I have been commanded to stay upon this beautiful island, yet there are many places I dream I could journey to. *I wish I could walk*

7. Despite setbacks and people who tell me my visions are impossible to achieve, I have never given up in the joy of dreaming in all its possibilities. *I wish I never stop dreaming*

Secrets the mountain never spoke aloud

Your Ink Speaks

When I am a fiery sky
zooming into your atmosphere
you'd know it is because
the flames of injustice being stoked
in the world push me to speak
in the voice I know is loud
even to my ears but is necessary

What each of us personally believes in
connects with and wants in their inner circle
should not become the scales of measurement
we place on other humans

Respect is lost in the rapture of zeal
I am learning how to constructively release
my anger by being vocal about it
on my social platforms. I must admit
initially, it took a lot of courage
but I do not mind now because I know
my voice and what I stand for

When I speak of nature
I am full of the ocean
Sometimes, it is calm and gives you
a sense of surrealism and fantasy
Sometimes, it is wild and takes you
into the depth of yourself

Reena Doss

There are also shallow versions of you
that will deepen if you know
how to give it all time

This is why:
As a writer, I must speak
As a lyricist, I must interpret the time
As a poet, I must be ready to reveal
what art in humanity
wishes to remain in secret

It is how we realize our darkness
and strive to be more in the light
of who we know we can be

Our shadows paint who we really are,

not what we think we are

∞

Love Notes

For You

Across The Miles

Dear Blue Rose,

I love our memories because it felt like sitting beside sunlight and dissolving into sunbeams of laughter.

Your mop of hair twisting around your neck, that dimple in your right cheek threatening to disappear, soon after our lips devoured each other before settling back into our normal lines of introspection.

When you are not with me, my hands feels empty of yours. And I wait for a pandemic, wars, and the unknotting of the obstacles to be done so I can refill them again with all the love I've been gathering in my heart to cover all those unpredictable times we've been torn apart by circumstances beyond our control.

I am no longer a princess. I am a Queen who has outgrown accepting the destruction of my spirit as a part of love. Fill me with the joy of this wonder shared between us always.

Yours

xoxo

My dream's reality

Adored

You and I
we are two hearts
that know
the value of freedom
the melting of space
and the power of words

I like how you try
to understand my mind

I notice the little things
but most of all
you

Can I keep you?

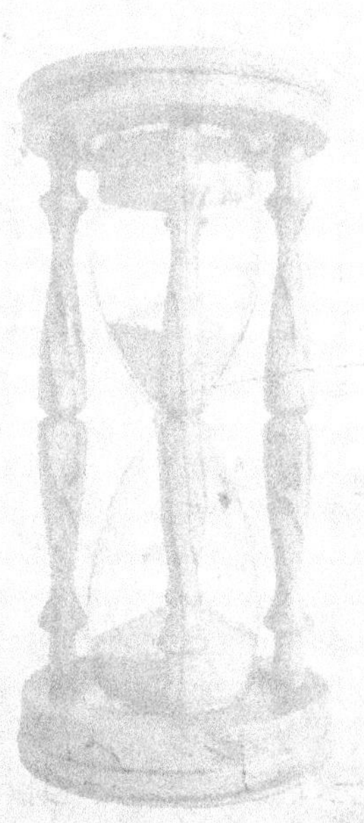

Reena Doss

Adventure

I wonder if
the Weaver heard my prayers
as I find safety in arms that know
how to hold all my unspoken words

And for the first time
I don't feel alone
in carrying its weight

I surrender to the string
that keeps me anchored—
the one that calls my name
encouraging freedom
that doesn't hold me back
but sets me free to fly endlessly
and my fear of being caged again
dissipates as my wings flutter in joy
my mind opens in waves
as my will yields in deference
like leaning back on a stranger's sofa
relaxing, instead of sitting on its edge
knowing I belong there

You're the adventure in all my adventures
that I dream of

∞

All Ours

When love is reluctantly given
or hidden, I drown the pain I feel
and send floods of love back into
the world, but now after all these years
I watch them come back to me
larger, bigger and overwhelmingly
all mine to soak in

I love this ocean within an ocean
within another ocean that found my own
It is in the encapsulation of my depth
that I recognize his

Our souls dance, our minds meld
but we are still learning
how to become one heart

And one day, we will become
one body when all the pieces
of our puzzle fit

The Weaver threads our tapestry

Reena Doss

A Lot

We are similar, yet we are not—
Extroversion versus Introversion

We exchange characteristics
in different aspects of our lives

How we get out of our heads:

You need the words and art of others
to mirror your thoughts
so you can find peace
from your data collection
of feelings that plague you

I need to write and create art for others
to mirror my thoughts
so they can find peace
from the emotional collection
of feelings that plague me

Sometimes, it is the other way
around for both of us
Being read by clever eyes
a wise soul and a kind heart
lets me feel seen

Such softness behind a cool exterior
can be intimidating to most
but not to me

I feel people's energies—absorb
and then reflect their aura;
it is why I am careful of who I let in

Experience has taught me
how to gauge
whether someone
energizes or drains me

After thinking things through
I realized that
it doesn't disconcert me any longer
though at first, I was shocked
on suddenly understanding
that someone else was
just as skilled at this ability
like I was

I like you more than a lot, a lot

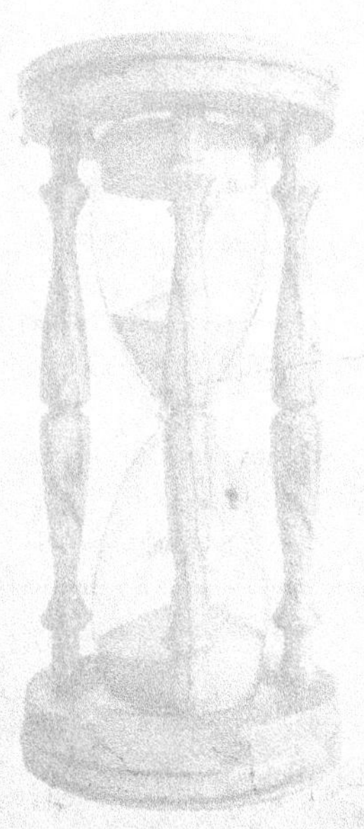

Reena Doss

Always

I've always been an always, always

Many want this type of certainty
but no one has had the courage
to make an effort to pursue it

No one. Until you

If you try to understand what I mean
without asking me what I mean
then you will never know what I mean

Ask me

Beloved

Love me like the Sun does
full of light from time to time
yet never ceasing in the dark
when the axis shifts each day
and I will love you like the Moon does
through all her constant phases

Devotion unwavering

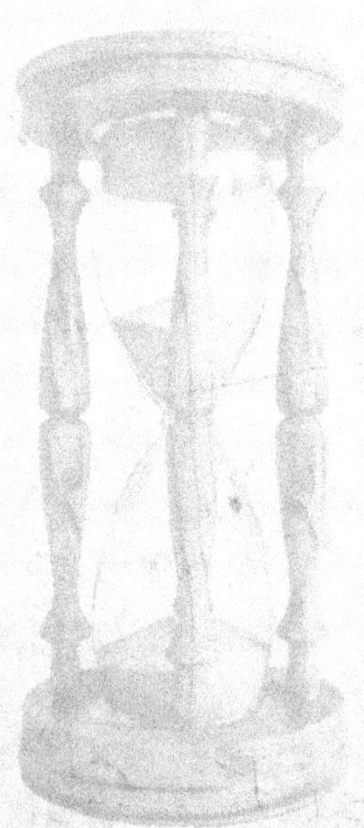

Reena Doss

Blind Man

And at last, I know what it's like
to have my truest self
touched by a blind man

I cannot find
enough words to describe
how intimate that is
or how a wish of mine
whispered to the King above
has come true

The contents of my spilling heart
are not misused but are understood
as shared tales of the dark
while I was searching
for eyes to see me

The blind man was given a sight
no one else had for he saw beauty
in my ashes, is a part of my growth
and has weathered through
the aftermath of the storms

As I come out of the nightmarish tunnel
where I was lost within, I see him with clarity
and feel my heart delight in his eyes

My own wander to his lips
and I think of things I probably shouldn't
because that is a whole other daydream in itself
But if a blind man can see so much
without being able to physically see me
what will happen when he can?
The entirety of my being trembles
at the very thought of experiencing
this depth of intensity with another
That is the intensity of depth I'm looking for
yet that is definitely the kind of man
I want to be with. I long to ask him
why he hasn't called yet. It is something
that I'd begun to believe may not exist in reality
Consistency colors the contents
of his heart in little moments for me
Time can be frustratingly slow
Time also moves so fast
Time drags its feet
when I want to race forward
One day, others will witness
how beautiful it can be
when a dazzling sunrise kisses
a blushing sunset on the horizon
where the Sky meets the Earth

The Weaver is still painting the full picture

Reena Doss

Boyfriend

Sometimes,
when I ponder the past—
the levels of betrayal
I was forced to accept
the layers of myself
I was asked to give up
and the heights of cruelty
I was subjected to
I feel sad about the girl
who I used to be

Then I think of you
and I smile
instinctively knowing
that I am in new skin
and that you are—
the obvious difference
from the rest
a rainbow palette
of colors,
the simple yet complex
exception

I think of you

∞

Breathe

"I want to love you
without having to keep thinking too much about it
I want to love you
like how people find breathing is", he said

"Then that's not loving, it's keeping me", I said

"No", he countered
"Breathing involves my entire body's cooperation
not just my lungs. It's the muscles that work ceaselessly
for my heart to pump its blood
so my mind feels bliss in your company
and my soul says, 'You're my forever girl'"

"Then why want something you already feel?" I asked

"Because, sweetheart, sometimes it gets hard to breathe"
he whispered softly

My Love

Reena Doss

Castle

When you need space, say it
rather than disappear
When you don't like something, speak up
rather than pretend you are fine with it

Learn how to talk about the tough stuff
Work out the difficulties together
There is no need for mind games
Be loyal in little things
Retrace your steps

I don't know about others
but I do not have a switch
that can just stop loving
I want it to keep growing—
yesterday, today, tomorrow
the day after and the many
others after that

That is how I love—
unconditionally
with no need to look around
for the exit

All the doors open to your touch

Come Closer

I told you about how I loved right from the start. I don't think you fully believed me, but strangely enough, I did not mind because I knew you would find out.

I wondered if you'd still want to keep diving in if I let you discover what you were searching for and so I unmasked myself for the first time.

Shocking myself, I broke down my own walls without hesitation once I knew I could, even though I questioned my own sanity frequently. I feared many times if you'd be disappointed if I told you that my dreams as a child have never changed.

I've never been the ambitious kind, though I've always wanted to make a difference in others' lives. I've never been interested in the corporate world though I've had to take up its banner to cover the ones who needed me. I've never wanted anything as much as I've wanted the grandest love story I could tell my grandchildren one day—safe arms that know how to keep expanding to hold everything about me, a home full of children's laughter, homemade smells emanating from the kitchen, and oodles of space to create the shapes that Hope, Faith and Love will take on each time I fill in its pages.

I like being old-fashioned—something that most modernized people I've come across condemn and dismiss as being too simple.

Reena Doss

I will never fit into a box because I know how to exist on both sides of it and will still choose the side that does not exist to others because I believe in the integrity of both—the masculine and the feminine existing in each of us.

I was burned out from drawing energy for years from the well that does not serve the essence of who I am—my femininity. It has awakened inside my body and I feel it reconnect with my heart and mind once more.

I love how easy it has started to become as I get guided by its continuous flow.

You are a planner, aren't you? I don't think most people have appreciated this side to you, but I will.

I will because then I can let go. I can let go of being so darned meticulous, cautious, and analytical; habits I picked up to protect those I love, but now seem more inclined towards self-preservation. They have suppressed the real parts of me and I don't like being this way.

I am ever flowing like a tap that can't be turned off. *I forgot to tell you not to open it.*

Water will transform itself into so many shapes to wrap itself around you in ways I am discovering it can.

∞

I am ever rising like a flame that can't be put off. *I didn't tell you to not to light the wick.*

Fire will seep over the sides from a volcano I didn't know existed till now.

I am ever evolving like the Earth that can't be siphoned off. *I couldn't tell you not to come closer because you already were a part of the story.*

Gardens, forests, and doors have begun to open from its rooted source—amplified by you stepping into my world.

I am full of songs, dreams, and magic

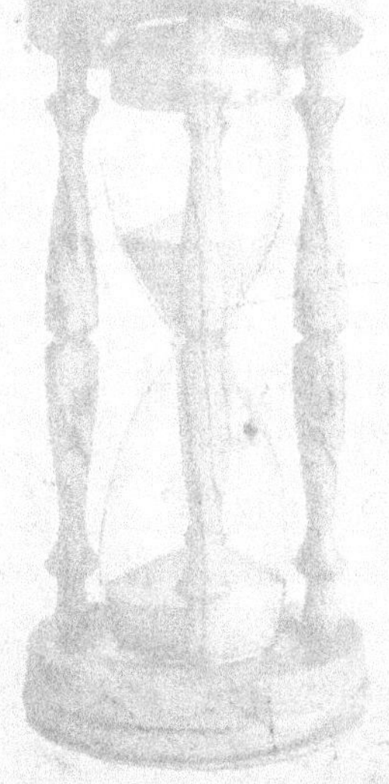

Reena Doss

Consistency

In all the time
she thought she was unlovable
do you know what it was like
for her to find out he loved her
but didn't tell her?

Do you know what it was like
for him to stay silent
because he feared he'd be
unlovable to her?

For though he'd heard
'I love you' multiple times
from other lips
he'd never felt them
make a home in his heart
until she said them

Making the words stick to you

∞

Continuous

You are a universe of poems
Watch as I create orbits
that spin so fast
it causes the world to feel dizzy
on learning the depth of your existence
wanting to know who it was
that unfroze a lost ocean
I don't let anyone in
but you walked in
with keys I couldn't help
giving you
An irresistible combination:
true kindness embodied in a gentleman
who had been taught the workings
of the sun and the moon
But your walls were so high
and I didn't realize I could
walk through them until I tried
to knock on your door
Then your universe overflowed
beckoning me to explore
the journey of your milestones

I had become water

Reena Doss

Deep

My feelings have never been shallow
Every nuance experienced
is submerged in waves of emotion
This is why I cannot maintain
surface interactions

This is why I lose those
who are not trustworthy
This is why I keep my true self
away from those who cannot see me

Honor is the only reason why I open
Loyalty is the only reason why I stay
Depth is the only reason why I connect

You remind me of my favorite heroes
hidden in my secret mind library
yet you are also not them at all

You are an original,
real and not fiction
and I'm so glad because
I could never feel this much
for someone superficial

Beyond the ground of the ocean

Into You

The words I want to tell you
are full of an Ocean's depth
They get dropped so shallowly
by those who do not know
how to measure its breadth

The words I want to tell you
are stuck on the tip of my tongue
I've only said them once before
to someone who didn't know
how to pour

The words I want to tell you
spill its secrets from my fingers
Memories of its first use
darken its trust in letting loose

The words I want to tell you
are ready to be spoken aloud
You've held my heart's pages
and stayed through the storms
despite the darkest clouds

The words I want to tell you
don't know how to stay still

Reena Doss

The waves flirt
with the shore's refined lines
as the Moon dances
with the Earth's window sill

The words I want to tell you
are caught between
a timid meep
and ecstatic roar

I don't know how to say them
I'm trying to give them wings

Eagle, teach them how to fly
The words I want to tell you are—
I love you

Sky and Mountain High

∞

Falling Star

Look at them on a boat
under the constellations
wishing that magic exists
hoping that our galaxies
can light the way
to pave a road for the lost

Let me fall and sink into the waters
as they sail toward their dreams

Maybe, I might be the one
to let them see
the world and us
from where we are

A wish for love

Reena Doss

Feathers

After the Sun told me who I was,
I awoke from under the heavy spell

He sent me a songbird,
who drew out all my raw beauty
in a way the world sees and enjoys
without ever knowing who found
the lost and wild ocean,
without ever knowing who stood by
as my rain was collected,
without ever knowing who waited
patiently to plant seeds of kindness
deep inside my broken heart
Look at how I unfurl and know
that it was you who helped me grow
by setting Hope free when you
uncaged my birds of Spring

Now when the meadows
open themselves to you,
I'm certain, Mountain,
that you will study
how to gently nourish
each facet of their becoming

I sing when he asks

For You

One day you'd tell me
all the words you want to say

I see how your demons
keep them stuck in your throat,
but your eyes soften
with unchecked feelings,
and you catch me,
as I fall,
as I run to you,
despite my own demons
threatening
to conquer my joy
in these moments

We fear losing what we know
yet do not know will stay
so I will let my heart remain
in the way it has always been
the day you knocked
and it opened on its own
without any resistance

My windows are always open

Reena Doss

Fruits

My heart has always been gentle
despite learning how to survive
in battlefields

I see myself
growing young with you
laughing about stupid things
we did and said
when we were too old
to know the difference
between the weight of living
with the angst of an adult
versus the beauty of living
with the heart of a child

Sometimes I ask the Weaver
what apple tree did I ask Him for?
And then I laugh
because books have always been
my best inspiration
for the greatest adventures
and you are all the best ones

I want to share things, celebrate joy and laugh with you

∞

Gentle Heart

Oh gentle heart
buried behind layers of masks
I hear your true voice
begging me to see the real you
Oh gentle heart
trusting your feelings is a challenge
I know your intelligent mind
seeks to understand mine
Oh gentle heart
your boundaries
have become high walls
I understand why you're afraid
to let me know
I'm already in

Oh gentle heart
I will paint for you to see

Oh gentle heart
I will write for you to know

Oh gentle heart
I will sing for you to believe

Oh gentle heart, your heart is meant for me

Reena Doss

Granted

All the loves we thought we lost
all the loves that left us lonely
hopeless and lying in the dark
searching and believing lies
that God had forgotten us—
our grand love story
our happily ever after ending
But now, I'm standing here with you
as a witness among witnesses
knowing with every beat of my heart
the truth of today—
the Weaver has done the impossible
what everyone, including us
doubted could be possible
for you see, my darling
nobody can steal or take the love
that He has created for us to find
Only we can stand in the way
of our happiness
if we give in to doubt and fear
instead of faith and trust
for in Him, all things
shall always be possible

A grand love story

∞

Knight

Look at how my voice flowers open
to speak in its freedom

No one else can understand
what empowerment can feel like
unless they had their wings
tortured into cruel submission
but you helped set them free

You might not have been a hero
in another's story
but you will always be
in mine

You rescued me

Reena Doss

Library

I've always enjoyed
books about heroes and heroines
visual creativity
poetry for lovers
coffee with concepts
tea with the rain
wine to celebrate
and revealing music
but I would like to add You
to the top of this list

I've always loved exploring libraries
and I hope you'd stay
to become
my favorite one

Please stay

∞

Like a Rose

How do you know
how to hold me so well?

I am not afraid of
feeling what's in my heart
or speaking my mind
or messing up

I am fighting unkind demons
but you cheer me on
as I battle them

You understand why I need to
You respect my ability to make it
You don't tell me what to do

When the demons come
you let me free
when I want to run
Memories of the past blind me
but these days, I don't want to run
so I face them with courage
because all I want to do
is run to the safe place
you created for me
right from the beginning

Reena Doss

because I bloom
like a flower
when I'm held by you
and one day, when what is
uncertain melts away
I'll tell the world
who it was that brought me
back to the living

You are the guardian of my heart

∞

Loved

"I have something to tell you", she told him, shaking and afraid.
He quietened and tuned in to the fear in her voice,
"What is it? You know you can tell me anything."

Swallowing hard, she decided to be fearless.
"If you choose to love me, you have to know it will be difficult",
she said in a matter-of-fact voice.

"Why?" he asked, worry wrinkling the lines on his brow
as he stared intently at her.

"Because... because I am not lovable", she told him in a rush,
like as if she was making the worst confession in the entire world.
"Oh, I know God loves me but I'm not really..."
she stammered to a halt, struggling to explain.

"Not... not lovable", he repeated, a bit stunned...
Then suddenly, he threw his head back and laughed
like she had told the biggest joke he'd ever heard.

Distracted by the way his face lit up when it was full of mirth,
she forgot to be anxious.
I like it when he laughs, she thought.

"This isn't funny!" she told him. "I'm serious."

Reena Doss

"Of all the things I expected you to say, that was never it",
he said, not bothering to stop laughing as he pulled her close.

Strangely, for some reason,
this comforted her more than any words,
though she couldn't help scowling at him.

Completely unfazed by her disgruntled frown,
he continued, grinning,
"Darling, I don't know why you believe in that nonsense
but if anything is going to be challenging for me,
it is to make you understand that you are.
Completely and utterly."

She looked at him then—
at how the stars found their way into his blues
that had turned into a passionate midnight,
at how the corners of his eyes crinkled in mirth,
and at how he held her so warmly.

And for the first time she knew she didn't just want to believe it—
she was on the edge of knowing that she was…

Lovable

∞

Meet

Two
Different nationalities
Met online
They spoke
For hours and hours
Until they decided
To finally cross borders
Light and dark
Equally unbalanced them
But it was love
That conquered all

A translated emoji poem on love

Reena Doss

Miracle

I can't tell you how exhilarating
how uplifting, how revolutionary
it feels to me that you listen
to the voices of my heart

You are the candle that opens
my heart to you and you take it
and let it become a wildfire
throughout the world

You are the blessing, the gift
the compliment and the love
that I hoped for
but never hoped

To find

∞

Obsessed

I like the healthy version
of being obsessed
It's different from fixations

Being crazy about someone
should be about exploring their depth
the details and definitions
of what makes them who they are

It is that delightful combination
of curiosity and yearning
that keeps a connection young

I want that with only you

Reena Doss

One Day

Tangled thoughts
tied up tongue

Gazes so fierce
it rocked our beings
scorching heat
and passionate highs

Overwhelming emotions
flooding hearts

Kindness was the molding tool
when only vulnerability
were the clothes we chose
to wear over our defenses

When hearts know a secret

∞

Orb

You surf
so beautifully over my waves

How do you know the ways
of the wind and the sea?
What tools did you acquire
on your journey underwater?

Have you fallen from the Sky
oh Celestial Heart?

You are a moving body of light

Reena Doss

Paintbrush

You are a riot on wheels
painting a kaleidoscope of colors
on the off chance it brings magic
by dancing a moon jig
under a bright red umbrella
inside a summer dandelion

You are art itself

Paradox

Were I but a full map
I would be whole
but what fun is there
in the hunt for treasure?

I'm pieces of the same map
and we put them together
until we have the whole picture
for you are many voices speaking
and I am many women rising

Kiss every piece

Reena Doss

Path

All I'm conscious of is
that with you—
I don't want to lead
I don't want to run
I don't want to hide
and so I tear open my heart
for your eyes to witness
the parts of me
I do not share
with anyone—
the heavy, the broken
and the shattered…
Observe well the worst—
I've unveiled all the scars
the world made me feel ugly for
There is nothing dark to process
or secrets hidden any longer
I can now answer questions
without fear guarding my tongue
anxiety keeping me on edge
and panic stalling my responses
I wish you understood
how completely strange it is
for me to spill so much ink
from clogged and frozen sections
beneath the rocks
of my ever-flowing rivers

∞

I know it's because
I want you to learn the routes
in my treasured maps
so you'd never be afraid of drowning
but will float, flow and fly
upon their timeless journey
of unstructured waves
directed steadily towards
my concealed ocean of ink
This is why I fought
to free myself
from being chained for years
with words not disclosed
to any man
until you came along
You could walk away
if you wanted to
after I showed you me
but it is a risk I took
because for the first time
in my life,
I want to speak
I want to be seen
I want to give in

To you

Reena Doss

Perfect

I only want
his hands in mine

They would be
the perfect stars to hold
for all time

Take my hands

Plea

In the whispers of the night
towards the early morn
of a western sky,
I hear these words
come out of nowhere,
a bit hazy yet it stumps me
for more than a millisecond:
If you could choose,
which storm is the greater?
To answer that is simple
yet complex
Always the last one,
I reply

Many storms have descended
but dark storms have come my way
over these long years, each one
more baffling and destructive
than the prior ones
and when I escaped
the last heaviest one…
I asked the Sun
I asked the Sun
I asked the Sun

Please, please, please send a Knight my way

Reena Doss

Quiet

Can you hear it?

The silence in the way we move
ridiculously simple—
we breathe in sync

Can you feel it?

Complexity
Growth
Healing

Can you see it?

Rainbows

Rainbows are born
when the bad storms burst
into a heart that opens itself
to absorb yours

Rainbows are born
when the rain falls heavily
onto their own skin
which pushes out
aged bottles of blue ink
they once stored in the attic
through their fingers

Rainbows are born
when the sun comes out
to wrap itself around lovers
in a technicolor prism of love
that only they know
belongs to them

The sky looks good on you

Reena Doss

Tasting

To taste the essence of my soul
is to receive me
and I will protect you
with my mind, my heart
and my body

I don't do things in half-measures
I'm either present or I'm not

To taste the essence of your soul
is to hold you close
without leaving you

The wine of your voices

Waiting

I don't love easily but when I do
you will never be a fickle moment
a simple thought or a boring
cacophony of sound

You will be a new day
to walk with every day
even on days when the not-so-nice storms
come to rock the comfortable sailing boat
a house to express the seven seasons
that I'll tell you all about some day
and a love I've nurtured carefully
for more than two decades
with the Weaver waiting patiently
to pour into every facet of your being
ever since the stars and I knew a secret

I save moments
because I crave exclusivity
with the one made for just me

Don't stop walking towards me

Reena Doss

Wild

I had learned from experience
that the process of love
does not always land in forever
because of its constantly
shifting names and changing faces

Perhaps the journey
of love in itself
is an everlasting mysterious
and unwinding road

For how is it possible
that our lifelines—
bridged so many miles apart
still sought, formed
and drew us together
into a wild shaped heart?

Your heart was meant for me

∞

Wolf Howl

Tossed into the winds of change
lost in many worlds you call your own
You are afraid to belong
though you were born to lead
in a destiny not quite clear yet

Courage worn armor
battle made steel
you protect the weak
with strength of equal will

Ready to defend your pack
if called upon
teeth barred, deadly snarl
to those who threaten your family

Confused about your place
searching for peace
playing many parts
you follow the emblem
of your house, your heart
and true north creed—
love before all

Your lone wolf howls in the distance
hearing the cries of your chosen mate

Reena Doss

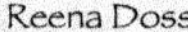

Eager to find me under the silver moon
we are constantly separated and reunited
by many unknown forces
You brave the storms to shut down
pride and ego to call this love yours

Like the fierce and resilient
chasing back and forth waves
that run to embrace the shore
you capture my heart
as it stabilizes your own

Finding your life partner

∞

World

Your languages
are the same as mine
though used differently

Teach me their grammar
and pronunciations
so I can teach you mine

I'm familiar
with their traversed paths
but now speak it
with the only other being
that seems to understand
their secrets

I am falling in love with your countries

Reena Doss

Unending

You are the Sky
carrying unheard stories
You are unheard stories
weaving many dreams
You are many dreams
falling deeply for the Earth
You are the Earth
absorbing all the rain
You are the mountain, wild eagle
lion, wolf, and bear
You are arms filled with
excitement, safety and warmth
You are so much more
than what I can see
and only an ocean can hold you
so come rain in me
There has never been
a beginning or an end
ever since our souls met

You and I

∞

Unfettered

Today, I'm the sea
tomorrow I'll be the tree—
but what I'm trying to say
is that I want to be
as free as the way I feel

When I'm with thee

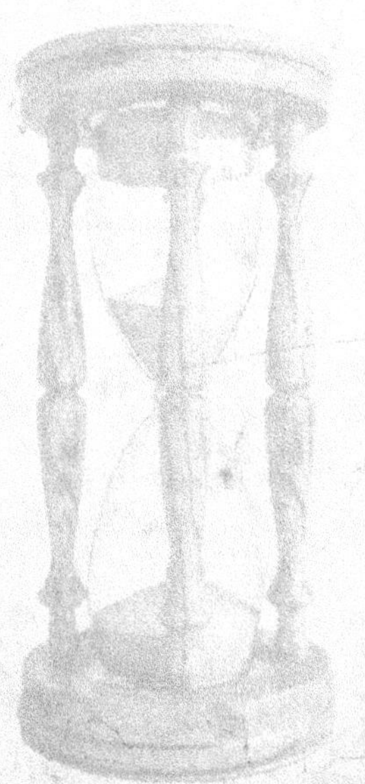

Reena Doss

Untamed Storm

More than lightning
as it streaks across the sky
I understand thunder
for the sound tears my heart
as it reveals your pain

Surrenders in ink

Us

You hold yourself back
because you are naturally meticulous
but when I trust-fall, you catch me

You are not usually so certain
because you prefer being analytical
but when I unravel, you understand me

You wonder about the depth of my waters
and that's why you value caution
but when I invite you in
you dive without hesitation
and this is why I hope…

Your eyes will look into mine

Your hands will capture mine

Your heart will claim mine

Reena Doss

Yours and Mine

You and I work too hard at love
when we are the cosmic formula
that proves its existence

You are the kind of man
who will unapologetically climb my walls
see all the dreams and wishes I hide
in there and claim them as yours

I'm the kind of woman
who will rip open your heart
see all the love and care
you hide in there
and claim them as mine

I am unabashedly indifferent
to your pretended indifference
Many say that's how I get hurt
but ask me to love any other way
and I will fail quite happily

One day, your heart will rise with mine
from the ashes of these long days and nights

You see me unlike any other

∞

Your Soul

I want to ask you
questions about your fire
things that confuse and puzzle
things that make me wonder
like why the sun and moon shine together
and laugh when in my sight

And even though I love
the romance of signs
because it gives that feel-good vibe
I don't base the growth
of my feelings in them
because I put my faith
in the promise the Weaver gave me
even when nothing makes sense
or I go through doubt

I want to know more about you

Reena Doss

Acknowledgements

I am grateful

A simple act of kindness may ignite the truth of what light is to someone in a palace with everything, more than to a homeless soul with not a penny to his name. And at the same time, the warmth of fire, a good meal and a roof may mean more to a homeless soul than it does to someone who already has all these things. But there is a third side not many admit unless they are brave enough to.

Love means everything to each of us and how it is given and received is how we enter the world and touch all we meet. Let us stand over borders, join in revolutions to right wrongs and connect hands instead.

This is why I wish to thank *my Beloved Weaver* who safeguards, guides and protects my heart for the one who is imperfectly perfect for me. You see, that is my big dream.

Thank you also to the *Love Of My Life* wherever he is sitting right now and who I know will one day come to claim the moon heart he worked so hard to understand. Thank you for saying, "I know you. You are going to do it because you're you. You've got this." Sometimes, words like that offer the type of hand you are looking for to guide you closer to your path of big dreams.

A special thank you to *Shruti Sharma* for accepting my request to read **In-Betweens,** my second volume of The Charcoal Diaries. I know it wasn't possible for you to edit the full manuscript, but thank you for being there at the start of it draft of a few pages.

Thank you for being one of the few who gave me their time during the in-betweens when I wanted to hear the voice of someone who cared say what I didn't know I needed.

Thank you Magic Megan and Brandy Lane for proofreading the original draft of a few pages as well, and for being a part of the first three Charcoal Diaries' adventures.

I am also grateful for all the workshops I attended during this period of time, including Miriam Otto's creative book workshops—Wild Fire and Magic, prompts as well as the Amsterdam Workshop— Writing for Peace.

Thank you to all *the founders, leaders, curators and team members of the communities, organizations and groups on Instagram,* for helping voices all over the world to transform, grow and create in a safe place during different seasons. You never stop inspiring me through your actions to continue to be a beacon of strength, solidarity and solace to all those struggling to find their light in the dark.

With a grateful heart, waves of hope and so much love,

Reena Ross

Reena Doss

About the author

Writing is Reena Doss' first voice of expression, followed closely by art and creativity. Through the encouraging platform provided by the Instagram community, she reclaimed her lost voices, evolved a few others and discovered new ones along the way. This has redeemed her trust that consistent Hope, Faith and Love in what is true ignites what is impossible to occur. Her adoration for her beloved Weaver, the Celestial Sky, Nature and her fellow Earthians has given her immeasurable courage to endure every season with a resilience born from battles overcome.

Born in Calcutta with roots drawn from Chennai and Pondicherry, Reena Doss has lived most of her life in the south of India—Bangalore. Though she prefers traveling to far-off places inside her head, she sometimes ventures into the world that others call real.

You can try and catch her but it may not always be possible as she is generally off on adventures flying on phoenix wings, swimming into the deep with mermaids and chasing fiery dragons down for stories.

Please scan the following QR code to follow her
on Instagram @reenadossauthor

www.reenadoss.com

I'll find you in the dark because I'm the girl
who loves to stay lost amongst the midnight stars,
caught up with moonbeams in a lantern,
trying to find my way back home.

Reena Doss

Ink Gladiators Press®

Publishing and promoting warriors on life's battlefield

We serve the community of creatives as a whole. We love to publish, promote and preserve the voices of authors, writers, artists, poets, lyricists, photographers, philosophers, editors, designers, storytellers, mental health advocates, communities and creators.

Our aim is focused on a vision where authors, professionals and creatives can grow together by contributing their heart songs to humanity as gifts of inspiration where reality can be built through the art of dream-making.

Thank you for being here.

We remain at your service,
Ink Gladiators Press® Team
www.inkgladiatorspress.com

For any inquiries, please email us at contact@inkgladiatorspress.com

Instagram | Facebook | Twitter
YouTube | Pinterest | Goodreads | LinkedIn

Please scan the QR Code below to follow us
on Instagram @inkgladiatorspress

Perhaps that is why only a Wolf can know

how the day greets the hawk

with the songs of the soul

www.reenadoss.com

www.ingramcontent.com/pod-product-compliance
Lightning Source LLC
LaVergne TN
LVHW020007110526
838588LV00033B/549